AF334400

PATHWAY TO PRAYER

קונטרס עבודת התפלה

A Translation and Explanation of all the Amidah Prayers of Shabbos

Plus
excerpts from
Practical Halachos
of Shabbos

Rabbi Mayer Birnbaum

Please send any comments or corrections to:

Rabbi Mayer Birnbaum
79 Reid Ave.
Passaic, N.J. 07055
973-778-8536

Cover design: *Bottom Line Design* *718-377-4567*
Distributed by: *Feldheim Publishers* *800-237-7149*

This sefer *is dedicated*

In honor of

הרב המחבר שליט״א

by

Mr. and Mrs. Dovid Spector

(Passaic, N.J.)

אלעזר מנחם מן שך

קרית הישיבה

בני - ברק

הנה ראיתי מאת הרה"ג היקר מהורר"ר מאיר הלוי בירנבוים שיחי' **קונטרס**
"עבודת התפלה" אשר בו מבאר ומפרש כל מילה ומילה מתפלת שמונה עשרה שלא יהי'
ח"ו מהדברים העומדים ברומו של עולם ובני אדם מזלזלין. וכל מה שפירש וביאר
ממקורות מוסמכים. ואף שגודל מעלת התפילה מבואר בחז"ל אבל כמה ההרגל גורם
שנאמר התפילה כמתעסק ובלא כוונה ובמהירות וחושב שיוצא ידי חובתו. לזה הוא בא
לעורר ולהסביר שכל אחד ואחד ימצא בו יותר מהחיוב לתת עיונו בתפלה. וכאשר נוכחתי
לדעת שהדברים יוצאים אך ורק לשם שמים **בודאי יכנסו בלב כאו"א וישפיעו הרבה.**

ואשאר בברכה מרובה שיזכה שיפוצו דבריו ברבים ויתקבלו.

מנאי המכבדו ומוקירו

אלעזר מנחם מן שך

Approbation of the
Sage of the Generation, *Maran*
Hagaon R' Elazar M. M. Shach *zt"l*

(Translated from the approbation to the Hebrew edition)*

I have seen the ***Kuntres Avodas Hatefillah*** by Rabbi Mayer Birnbaum, in which he explains and translates each and every word of the prayer of *Shemoneh Esray*, so that it should not be among those exalted things that people treat lightly, God forbid. Everything that he translated and explained is from reliable sources. Even though the greatness of prayer is explained in the words of the Sages, the habitual recitation of prayer causes one to pray as if he were preoccupied, saying it quickly and without concentration, yet thinking that he has fulfilled his obligation. For this reason, the author has come to inspire and to explain the obligation of every single person to pray with greater concentration. And since I know that the author is publishing these words solely for the sake of Heaven, they will surely enter the heart of every individual and will have a great influence.

I close by giving a great blessing that the author's words should be widely spread and accepted.

From me, who honors and respects him,

Elazar Menachem Mann Shach

---

* The Hebrew edition does not include the section of "Practical Halachos of Shabbos"

Haskamah to *Pathway to Prayer — Shemoneh Esray*

אברהם פאם
RABBI ABRAHAM PAM
582 EAST SEVENTH STREET
BROOKLYN, NEW YORK, N. Y.
11218

בס״ד

הנה הרה״ג ר׳ מאיר בירנבוים שליט״א נתעורר על נחיצות הענין לתרגם ולפרש את תפלת שמונה עשרה. דברתי קצת עם המחבר בעניני תרגום וראיתי שמדקדק טובא. וגם כבר איתמחי גברא בחיכורו ״קונטרס עבודת התפלה״ שנתקבל ברצון בעולם התורה, ועכשיו בא לתרגם את ספרו לאנגלית לצורך אלו שקשה להם להבין לשון הקודש.

הנה באמת זהו ענין חשוב מאד לרומם ערך התפלה שעיקרה עבודה שבלב, ובודאי ספר זה יעזור שיהיו התפלות נאמרות יותר כתיקונן.

(Translation of the Hebrew)

Rabbi Mayer Birnbaum has realized the importance of translating and explaining the prayer of *Shemoneh Esray*. I have spoken a little with the author concerning the translation of prayer and I have seen that he is very meticulous. The author has already established his reliability through his *Kuntres Avodas Hatefillah* that has been warmly received in the Torah world, and now he has translated his work into English for those who have difficulty understanding Hebrew.

Indeed this is a very important endeavor, to elevate the stature of prayer which is primarily a service of the heart, and this work will surely help people pray more meaningfully.

Avrohom Yaakov Hakohen Pam

בס"ד

Rabbi Meyer Birnbaum has enriched the Jewish world of prayer with his works illuminating the prayers. His concise comments and guide to the meaning of the prayers have been accepted and are used universally.

Rav Birnbaum has now undertaken to provide an English version of his inspiring works. We are deeply grateful to him for doing so.

The English version will enable a wider range of Jews involved in service of Hashem to benefit from the mind opening guides of this gifted work.

With deepfelt blessings to the author and deep longing for the ultimate service in the Beis Hamikdosh.

Rabbi Yaakov S. Weinberg
Rosh HaYeshiva

YSW:mg

Table of Contents

Preface

I thank Hashem with all my heart for having granted me the opportunity to present this *sefer* (book) *Pathway to Prayer — Shabbos* to the English-speaking public. This volume is the third in a series of *Pathway to Prayer*. The previous volumes, one on the daily *Shemoneh Esray* and one on the Rosh Hashanah and Yom Kippur *tefillos* (prayers), have been very well received, and many have asked that I continue this series, especially concerning the Shabbos prayers.

This volume is basically a translation of the Hebrew work that I published *b'ezras Hashem* several years ago — **Kuntres Avodas Hatefillah** on *Shabbos* — which elucidates every phrase of the *amidah* prayers of this very holy day. This *sefer* has been enthusiastically received both in Israel and in America (already in its fifth edition) and I hope that this English version will allow a wider audience to benefit from this concise, practical work. My goal is that it should provide those who want to improve their Shabbos *tefillos* with a deeper understanding of those special prayers, and thereby enhance their entire Shabbos, both in spirit and in action.

Since on Shabbos people often have some free time either before or after their prayers, I thought it would be beneficial to add some excerpts from a book that I recently published, **Practical Halachos of Shabbos**. Although it is recommended to read through that work in its entirety, I have included at the end of this *sefer* some very relevant *halachos* (laws) which the reader will surely find enlightening.

I began the format of these works while still a student in the Yeshiva of Staten Island and since then it has grown to an entire set that covers all the Amidah prayers of the entire year. I want to take this opportunity to thank the *Menahalim* and *Rabbeim* of the Yeshiva of Staten Island for having taught me the ways of the Torah, and for having guided me from the day I came to the yeshiva (over 20 years ago) until this day. A special *hakoras hatov* (gratitude) is due to my Rebbe, Rabbi Moshe Boruch Newman, *shlita*, for all his encouragement, guidance, and patience. It is impossible to describe how much I have gained from him. Also, I owe a special *hakoras hatov* to the *Mashgiach*, Rabbi Chaim Mintz, *shlita*, who has been a tremendous encouragement particularly since I left the Yeshiva, and who has been of special guidance to me in my current position as *Mashgiach* in the Yeshiva Gedolah of Bayonne.

It was also a great privilege to be together every summer in the yeshiva's camp with the *Rosh Hayeshiva, Maran Hagaon* **Rav Moshe Feinstein**, *zt"l*.

Being in the presence of the *Gadol Hador* for the entire summer left an indelible impression on all of us. Watching his every action, especially how he stood during *tefillah* like a servant before his Master, one could learn what it means to be a true servant of Hashem.

Also, a special *hakoras hatov* is due to my dear friend, Rabbi Shimon Shain, *shlita,* who has been a *chaver tov* in the true sense of the words (see *Rabbainu Yonah* on *Avos 1:6*). His inspiration and friendship have been, and are, a great *chizuk* for me. May he have *siyata di'shmaya* to continue growing in Torah and *Yiras Shomayim*, and may he share his wellsprings of Torah with many others.

I also want to express my great appreciation to Yeshivas Ner Yisrael in Baltimore, where I studied in *kollel* for nine years. I benefited greatly from being there, especially while the *Rosh Yeshiva, Hagaon Horav* Yaakov Yitzchok Ruderman, *zt"l,* was still giving *shmuezen (mussar* discourses), and from the many private conversations I had with this *gadol.* Also, the quiet example of care and concern of the great *askan*, Rabbi Naftali (Herman) Neuberger, *shlita,* left an indelible impression on me.

I would also like to express my gratitude to the Yeshiva Gedolah of Bayonne where, together with the *Rosh Hayeshiva*, Horav Dovid Magid, *shlita,* I have merited to teach Torah for several years. May Hashem grant us the strength to continue to teach and glorify His Torah.

A special thanks to Rabbi Yitzchok Penfil and Mrs. T. Finkelman whose skillful editing has tremendously improved this work.

Of course, I owe a tremendous *hakoras hatov* to my parents, Rabbi and Mrs. Naftali Birnbaum, *shlita,* for bringing me up to appreciate Torah and *Tefillah.* Their encouragement and help in everything has enabled me to reach thus far, *b'ezras Hashem.* I would also like to thank my parents in-law, Rabbi and Mrs. Reuven Shnidman, *shlita,* for their encouragement in all my projects. May Hashem bless them all with long life in good health and much *Yiddishe Nachas* from all their children and grandchildren.

And last, but certainly not least, my great appreciation and *hakoras hatov* to my wife Rochel, whose tireless efforts, selflessness and encouragement have enabled me to spend the countless hours that it took to complete this work. May Hashem give us *siyata di'shmaya* to serve Him properly and bless us with much *Yiddishe Nachas* from all of our children.

Mayer Birnbaum
Marcheshvan 5763 / October 2002

Introduction

Praised is the Creator Who gave us the special day of Shabbos, which the *Gemara* (*Shabbos* 10b) calls a great gift. Shabbos is "a sign between Me and the *Bnei Yisrael*," a sign that we are His chosen nation, for He made His day of rest our day of rest (*Rashi, Shemos* 31:13).

The *Mishnah Berurah* [written by the *Chofetz Chayim*, R' Yisrael Meir Kagan (1838-1933)] wrote in his introduction to the Laws of Shabbos the following: Shabbos is the foundation of our belief that the universe was created from nothing*, and since God created everything He is the Master of everything and we are His servants and are obligated to do His will and to serve Him with all our lives and possessions, for everything is His. And the Sages tell us that anyone who keeps Shabbos is considered as if he fulfilled the entire Torah, and anyone who desecrates Shabbos is considered as if he denies the entire Torah, because Shabbos is the foundation of our belief.**

All the days of the week a person is busy with his affairs and does not have time to think. Therefore Hashem gave the Jewish people the great present of Shabbos in order for them to be free from their occupations to cling to the Creator of the world and to comprehend the

---

* *Kuzari* [R' Yehuda HaLevi (1075-1141)] (1:57) writes an interesting proof of the creation of the world. Have you ever heard of any country that argues with the seven-day week, which begins on Sunday and ends on Shabbos? Is it possible that there should be such unanimity among the people of China and the people of Portugal (or the Canary Islands) concerning the days of the week, without an original agreement? Obviously, the reason they all have the same seven-day week — a rather unusual number — is that it all started with the first man, Adam, who knew that Hashem created everything in six days, and rested on Shabbos. So we see that the set-up of our calendar is proof of the creation of the world.

** Any person with a clear mind can, with just a little thought, recognize that the world was created by God. It is so simple that every boy, when he reaches the age of bar mitzvah (13), and girl, when she reaches bas mitzvah (12), is obligated to believe this. As R' Elchonon Wasserman (1875-1942) wrote, belief that God created the world is obvious to anyone with intelligence, as long as he is not a fool, for how can any intelligent person say that the entire world came about by itself, after seeing tremendously deep, endless wisdom in every little thing. How much wondrous wisdom is there just in the human body, as any doctor or surgeon will testify! How could anyone say that such a marvelous machine happened by itself without any

truth of the creation of the world. R' Yaakov Tzvi Mecklenburg [famous 19th cent. author of the *Ksav ve'Hakabalah*] wrote in his commentary on the *siddur* (Shabbos *Minchah*): One should know that the cessation of work that the Torah demands on Shabbos is not in order to give a rest to the body from the toil and exertion of the weekdays, as is commonly thought; rather, one must realize that the true intention of the rest from work on Shabbos is to allow the soul to rest and enjoy the serenity to think about spiritual matters, to free one's mind for thoughts of Torah, which will elevate him to recognize the greatness of the Creator, Praised be He.

In addition to the actual present of a day of rest, Hashem gives us an additional present every Shabbos. The *Gemara* (*Beitzah* 16a) says that every *Erev Shabbos* (before Shabbos) Hashem gives a Jew a *neshamah yeseirah* — an additional soul — and on *Motza'ay Shabbos* (after Shabbos) He takes it from the person. What is the purpose of this *neshamah yeseirah*?

The *Sforno* [R' Ovadiah Sforno (1470-1550)] writes (*Shemos* 20:11): "The *neshamah yeseirah* gives one additional preparation to serve Hashem." Further, he writes (*Shemos* 31:17), "It is an extra degree of spirituality to enable one to achieve the level that Hashem intended for him to reach by making man in His image." We see from

---

thought of a designer? If someone would tell you that a watch made itself, you would consider him insane; if so, how foolish are those who say that the entire world came about by accident! (*Dugma'os Le'beuray Agados* Ch. 1)

I would like to cite a more modern refutation to the absurd theory that some believe, that a human being came about by itself. The following is a quote from *Permission to Believe* [Lawrence Keleman, Targum Press 1990] (p.60-61): "There is only a 1 in $10^{39,950}$ chance that a single viable bacterium [a simple form of life] ever evolved on Earth. Remember: This is after we take into account a billion years' worth of trials. ... Nobel laureate [Dr. Fred] Hoyle calculated that these odds constituted "[such] an outrageously small probability that [it] could not be faced even if the whole universe consisted of organic soup." Hoyle added that *it was more likely that "a tornado sweeping through a junkyard might assemble a Boeing 747 from the materials therein."* And these are the odds of just a single bacterium randomly evolving. The odds of several bacteria evolving are worse, and the probabilities that a virus or fungus would evolve are simply comical. What about people? There are 25,000 operative enzymes in a human being (in contrast to a bacterium's 2,000). The probability of 25,000 enzymes forming spontaneously once in a billion years is about 1 in $10^{599,950}$. In other words, the chances *of just the enzymes* in a person evolving randomly sometime in Earth's history are the same as the chances of pulling one red marble out of a mound of black marbles *trillions and trillions and trillions of times larger than the entire universe, in one try.* And this is not to mention assembling those

here that Shabbos was endowed with the special qualities which each person needs to attain spiritual perfection.

Reishis Chochmoh [R' Eliyahu di Vidosh (16th cent.)] (*Sha'ar Kedushah* Ch. 3) explains further what is expected of our *neshamah yeseirah*: "Since Shabbos is special because of the *neshamah* that is added on that day, it is proper that we make the *neshamah* the important part of Shabbos. The main things that this *neshamah yeseirah* should accomplish are to **pray with more concentration** and learn a new portion of Torah." We see from this that one of the primary purposes of the *neshamah yeseirah* is to inspire us to *daven* (pray) better.

Panim Yafos [R' Pinchos Halevi Horowitz (1730-1805)] (*Parshas Yisro*) derives this from the *Gemara* (*Shabbos* 113b) that states: "One's speech on Shabbos should not be like one's speech during the week." He explains that this can not only mean that one should not talk about business on Shabbos [which is also included in this], for if so the *Gemara* would have said "One should not speak about weekday matters on Shabbos." Rather, it means that those words that one says on Shabbos just as he does during the week — namely, learning and prayers, particularly the first three *berachos* of the *Shemoneh Esray* which are identical on Shabbos and weekdays — those same words should be said on Shabbos with greater holiness. So we see that one must pray on Shabbos with greater concentration than he does during the week.

We ask in each Shabbos prayer, "... let our rest be pleasant before You." How could one ask this of Hashem, if he spends his entire Shabbos merely relaxing and not doing what the *neshamah yeseirah* was given for — that is, concentration in *tefillah* and learning Torah? Therefore someone who sincerely wants Hashem to be pleased with his rest on Shabbos should bear in mind the true purpose for which Shabbos was given.

---

enzymes into skin, bones, muscles, eyes§, noses, and ears, or assembling nucleotides into a strip of human DNA. The number $10^{599,950}$ is incomprehensibly large. ... The universe ... contains only about 10^{80} atomic particles. *Impossible* is only barely too strong a word to describe an event with a probability of 1 in $10^{599,950}$. Yet these odds are one of the most liberal estimates offered by scientists today."

§ Charles Darwin himself wrote in a letter, "The eye, to this day, gives me a cold shudder" (quoted in *Beyond a Reasonable Doubt,* by Rabbi S. Waldman, Feldheim Publishers 2002; p. 238). It should have, although certainly Darwin, the disbeliever, did not know of the phenomenal complexity of the eye as we know it today. The eye makes it crystal clear that there is a Creator!

Sforno makes a similar comment on the verse in the Ten Commandments (*Devarim* 5:12): "Keep the day of Shabbos to sanctify it like Hashem commanded you." He writes that Hashem made it known to you that it does not suffice to make Shabbos holy by resting from your work, but that you should be busy on it with Torah and *mitzvos* like He commanded you in *Marah* [see *Shemos* 15:25-26].

It is possible that this is why we follow "let our rest be pleasant before You" with the requests "make us holy so that we should do Your *mitzvos* properly, and give us Divine assistance that all of our occupation should be in Torah study," for the true way to make our rest pleasing to Hashem is through these two things — Torah and *mitzvos* — and therefore we ask for them immediately so that we should be able to achieve our perfection.

Pathway to Prayer

Shabbos

מעריב לשבת
Maariv for Shabbos

Master of all — in particular, My Master [1]   אֲדֹנָי

please open my lips (because I am afraid and ashamed to open them)   שְׂפָתַי תִּפְתָּח

and [help me pray with concentration, so] my mouth will [be able to] tell Your true praise.   וּפִי יַגִּיד תְּהִלָּתֶךָ.

אבות
Our God and the God of Our Fathers, Who Created Everything, and Protected Abraham[2]

You are the source of blessing (an expression of praise)[4]   **בָּרוּךְ** אַתָּה[3]

Master of all (Who always was, is, and will be)   יהוה

the Master of all strength Who is able to do anything and Who takes care of us with Divine Providence   אֱלֹהֵינוּ

---

1. The *Mesillas Yesharim* [R' Moshe Chayim Luzato (1707-1746)] (ch.19) writes that a person should think about three things when he begins to pray. It is possible that these three thoughts are hinted at in these three phrases that introduce the prayer:
   (a) he is standing in front of *Hashem* - "Master of all"
   (b) the exaltedness of *Hashem* - "open up my lips because I am afraid"
   (c) the lowliness of man - "and help me tell Your true praise"

2. One must be very careful to concentrate when saying this *berachah*, because otherwise he does not fulfill his obligation to pray. In the time of the *Gemarah* one would have to repeat the *Shemoneh Esray* if he had not concentrated on it. Nowadays, however, when we are not sure that the second time will yield the proper concentration either, we do not repeat the *Shemoneh Esray*. However, the *Mishnah Berurah* [the authoritative *halachic* work, written by R' Yisrael Meir HaKohen (1838-1933)] (101:4) states that if one did not yet say ברוך אתה ה' at the end of this *berachah*, he can go back to אלהי אברהם and repeat from there with concentration, thereby rectifying his previous lack of concentration.

3. The *Bais Elokim* [R' Moshe ben Yosef Trani (1500 - 1580)] explains that we bow at the beginning and end of this *berachah* because it contains a summary of all the praises of *Hashem* and His all-encompassing powers which signify His Oneness. Recognizing this, we bow down to *Hashem* in humility.

4. See Appendix to Pathway to Prayer — *Shemoneh Esray* concerning the reason for this translation, rather than the common translation "blessed."

and the God Who took care of our Fathers with Divine Providence (and made a covenant with each of them) וֵאלֹהֵי אֲבוֹתֵֽינוּ

the God Who made a covenant with our father Abraham (who excelled in kindness) אֱלֹהֵי אַבְרָהָם

the God Who made a covenant with our father Isaac (who excelled in service of God) אֱלֹהֵי יִצְחָק

and the God Who made a covenant with our father Jacob (who excelled in learning Torah) וֵאלֹהֵי יַעֲקֹב

He is the Almighty (all power is His, especially in exercising the attribute of mercy) הָאֵל

Who is the Great One (all greatness is His, especially in exercising the attribute of kindness) הַגָּדוֹל

(and) He is the Strong One (all strength is His, especially in exercising the attribute of judgment) הַגִּבּוֹר

and He alone deserves to be feared (because no being has the ability to do good or bad except Him) וְהַנּוֹרָא

for He is the supreme God Who is the ultimate cause of everything אֵל עֶלְיוֹן

Who always does kindnesses that are purely good גּוֹמֵל חֲסָדִים טוֹבִים

and He recreates everything, constantly, every day וְקוֹנֵה הַכֹּל

and every day He recalls for our benefit the kindnesses performed by the forefathers וְזוֹכֵר חַסְדֵי אָבוֹת

and He constantly brings the Redeemer closer וּמֵבִיא גוֹאֵל

to the forefathers' childrens' children (even though the merit of the forefathers might already be used up) לִבְנֵי בְנֵיהֶם

for the sake of His Name (which will be sanctified at the time of the Redemption) לְמַעַן שְׁמוֹ

[and He will also bring the Redeemer] because of His great love for the Jewish people

בְּאַהֲבָה

On Shabbos Shuvah the following is added:

Remember us for life in this world (in order that we may earn the World to Come by doing *mitzvos* here)

זָכְרֵנוּ לְחַיִּים

King, Who desires life (and not death for a sinner, but rather that he should repent)

מֶלֶךְ חָפֵץ בַּחַיִּים

and write us in the Book of the Righteous, for life

וְכָתְבֵנוּ בְּסֵפֶר הַחַיִּים

for Your sake, in order that we may serve You

לְמַעַנְךָ

the Master of all strength Who is able to do anything and is the One Who apportions life to all

אֱלֹהִים חַיִּים

He is the King over all

מֶלֶךְ

Who is the Helper (to help one succeed)

עוֹזֵר

and the Savior (from trouble)

וּמוֹשִׁיעַ

and the Protector (to prevent trouble from coming)

וּמָגֵן

You are the Source of Blessing, Master of all

בָּרוּךְ אַתָּה יהוה

the Protector of Abraham (and because of Abraham He continues His protection over us). [5]

מָגֵן אַבְרָהָם:

גבורות

The Mighty Acts of God and the Revival of the Dead[6]

You alone are eternally Strong

אַתָּה גִּבּוֹר לְעוֹלָם

Master of all

אֲדֹנָי

---

5. The *Midrash* (*Shir Hashirim*, ch.4) quotes R' Brechya in the name of R' Yitzchok, who says that *Hashem* said to Abraham, "To you I have been one shield, but to your children I will be many shields," as it says (*Shir Hashirim* 4:4), "A thousand shields are hanging on him."

6. While reciting this *berachah* we should instill in ourselves perfect belief in the Revival of the Dead, one of the thirteen principles of faith outlined by the *Rambam* [Maimonides] (1135-1204).

You even revive the dead (which shows the
greatest strength, contradicting all laws of nature)

מְחַיֶּה מֵתִים אַתָּה

[and] You have an abundance of strength with
which to save

רַב לְהוֹשִׁיעַ

FROM *MUSAF* OF *SHEMINI ATSERES* UNTIL AFTER *MUSAF* OF THE FIRST DAY OF *PESACH*, SAY:

He causes the wind to blow (which aids evaporation, blows
clouds where they are needed, and facilitates all aspects of rain)

מַשִּׁיב הָרוּחַ

and He causes every drop of rain to fall on its desired place
(and for its designated function: to nourish or to flood, etc.)

וּמוֹרִיד הַגָּשֶׁם

He provides all the living with their food
and other needs in kindness (not because
they are deserving)

מְכַלְכֵּל חַיִּים בְּחֶסֶד

He revives the dead with great mercy
(searching for merits with which they
would deserve revival)

מְחַיֶּה מֵתִים בְּרַחֲמִים רַבִּים

He supports those who are falling (whether
physically, emotionally, or financially)

סוֹמֵךְ נוֹפְלִים

and He heals the sick from all types of illnesses
(even when doctors have given up hope)

וְרוֹפֵא חוֹלִים

and He opens the bonds of those who are
restricted (e.g., giving movement to our
limbs when we awaken)

וּמַתִּיר אֲסוּרִים

and He will keep His promise to those
sleeping in the dust (the dead), to
revive them.

וּמְקַיֵּם אֱמוּנָתוֹ לִישֵׁנֵי עָפָר

Who is like You (who can do as many mighty
deeds, which are infinite, even for one person)?

מִי כָמוֹךָ

— You, to Whom all mighty deeds belong! —

בַּעַל גְּבוּרוֹת

And who is comparable to You in even one of Your
mighty deeds (which are of the highest quality)?

וּמִי דוֹמֶה לָּךְ

You are the King over all   מֶלֶךְ

Who causes death and revival in many respects   מֵמִית וּמְחַיֶּה
(such as sleep and awakening, poverty and wealth)

and, like the sprouting of a seed, You bring the   וּמַצְמִיחַ יְשׁוּעָה
Salvation (the Revival of the Dead) [7]

ON SHABBOS SHUVAH THE FOLLOWING IS ADDED:

Who is like You, who has as much mercy on his   מִי כָמוֹךָ אַב הָרַחֲמִים
sons as You, the Merciful Father, have for us

(and) remembers His creatures, out of   זוֹכֵר יְצוּרָיו לְחַיִּים בְּרַחֲמִים
mercy, for life

And (from the mighty deeds that we   וְנֶאֱמָן אַתָּה לְהַחֲיוֹת מֵתִים
mentioned) we see that You are surely
trusted to revive the dead

You are the Source of Blessing, Master   בָּרוּךְ אַתָּה יהוה
of all

the Reviver of all the dead (from Adam   מְחַיֵּה הַמֵּתִים:
until the time of the Revival). [8]

---

7. This salvation refers to the Revival of the Dead, which is a major topic in this *berachah*. A similar expression is used in the *Shabbos* morning prayers (in one of the *berachos* before *Shema*) where it says "and no one is comparable to You, our **Savior**, for the Revival of the Dead" [R' Yehuda ben Yakar (13th cent.)].

 This *berachah*'s comparison of the Revival of the Dead to the sprouting of a seed (a comparison found also in *Kesuvos* 111b) is explained beautifully by *Dovair Shalom* (in *Siddur Otzar Hatefillos*): death is not the end of a person; rather, it is like the burying of a seed, which decomposes in the earth to produce a plant or tree. In the same way, Hashem causes death in order to bring a person back to life in a more glorious form than he had been originally. The *Tiferes Yisrael* [R' Yisrael Lipshitz (1782-1860)] *(Or HaChayim 2a)* mentions another analogy: The caterpillar crawls around for a short time and then enshrouds itself in a cocoon, which is really like a grave, where it decomposes; but after a few weeks, out comes a creature with beautiful wings that can fly thousands of miles —a butterfly!

8. Even though many bodies have decomposed over thousands of years, and some have been burned and their dust has been scattered, and others have drowned at sea, *Hashem* with His great might will recognize and recompose the bodies and return to them their original souls (*Yesod Veshoresh Ha'avodah*) [R' Alexander Ziskind of Horodna (1740-1794)].

קדושת השם

Holiness of God

You, Yourself, are holy (different and separate from everything)	**אַתָּה** קָדוֹשׁ
and Your Name (which comes from Your many acts) reveals holiness	וְשִׁמְךָ קָדוֹשׁ
and the holy ones — Israel [9]	וּקְדוֹשִׁים
constantly praise You, every day, forever	בְּכָל יוֹם יְהַלְלוּךָ סֶּלָה
You are the Source of Blessing, Master of all	בָּרוּךְ אַתָּה יהוה
the Almighty, Who is holier than all else.	הָאֵל הַקָּדוֹשׁ.

ON SHABBOS SHUVAH THE FOLLOWING IS SAID *INSTEAD* OF THE LAST LINE ABOVE:

the King Who is holier than all else.	הַמֶּלֶךְ הַקָּדוֹשׁ.

קדושת היום - בריאת העולם

Holiness of the Day - Creation of the Universe[10]

You separated the seventh day (Shabbos) from all the work days to testify to Your Name	**אַתָּה** קִדַּשְׁתָּ אֶת יוֹם הַשְּׁבִיעִי לִשְׁמֶךָ
for it (the seventh day) is the conclusion of the work of creation of the heaven and earth	תַּכְלִית מַעֲשֵׂה שָׁמַיִם וָאָרֶץ

---

9. The Jews are called a "holy nation" in many scriptural verses (e.g., *Shemos* 19:6, *Devarim* 7:6).

10. The *Gemara* (*Shabbos* 119b) says that whoever says ויכלו (the second paragraph here) in the Friday evening prayer is considered a partner with Hashem in the

and You blessed it with additional good (that one's soul is able to grasp more wisdom on it[11]) more than the other days

וּבֵרַכְתּוֹ מִכָּל הַיָּמִים

and You made it holy by commanding us a more severe abstention from work than any holiday

וְקִדַּשְׁתּוֹ מִכָּל הַזְּמַנִּים

and so it is written in Your Torah (*Bereishis* 2:1-3):

וְכֵן כָּתוּב בְּתוֹרָתֶךָ :

And the heavens and the earth were completed

וַיְכֻלּוּ הַשָּׁמַיִם וְהָאָרֶץ

as well as all their armies (the sun, moon, stars and angels in the heavens; the animals, fish, plants and people on earth).

וְכָל צְבָאָם :

---

creation of the world. The *Rishonim* (early commentators; 11th-15th cent.) asked, is it not belittling Hashem's greatness to ascribe to Him a partnership with humans?

The *Orchos Chayim* [R' Aharon HaKohen from Lunil (13th-14th cent.)] (*Hilchos Shabbos* p 61) and the *Kolbo* [unknown authorship] (Ch. 35) answer that the intention of the *Gemara* is that when one says ויכלו it is as if he is affirming everything that is written in the Torah concerning the creation of the world, as if he himself witnessed it and as if he himself participated in its creation. For this belief he is considered a partner in the creation.

The *Yesod Veshoresh Ha'avodah* says that the *Gemara* did not extol the virtue of the one who says ויכלו if he merely says the words. Rather it refers to someone who, as he says it, strengthens his belief in the Oneness of Hashem and that He created the entire universe, including endless numbers of spiritual worlds, in the six days of creation, and, as a result, instills in his heart tremendous joy in having merited to be in the holy portion of Hashem (i.e. His chosen nation) to serve Him by doing all His *mitzvos*.

11. It is written in the *Aseres HaDibros* [the Ten Commandments] (*Shemos* 20:11), "For in six days Hashem made the heavens and the earth, the sea and everything that is in it, and He rested on the seventh day, therefore Hashem **blessed** the day of Shabbos and **made it holy**." What do these terms refer to ?

Sforno explains: The purpose of the six days was so that a person should be similar to his Creator as much as possible, whether in deep thought, in learning or in free will, therefore He blessed the Shabbos with a *neshama yeseirah* [an extra measure of spirituality], and that is the additional preparation to serve Hashem! That is what is meant by the phrase "Hashem **blessed** the day" — He blessed it with an extra measure of spirituality so that we should achieve our purpose.

And the Master of all strength Who is able to do anything already completed by the seventh day

וַיְכַל אֱלֹהִים בַּיוֹם הַשְּׁבִיעִי

His work of the sixth day that He did

מְלַאכְתּוֹ אֲשֶׁר עָשָׂה

and He abstained on the seventh day

וַיִּשְׁבֹּת בַּיוֹם הַשְּׁבִיעִי

from all the work He had done all the six days of creation.

מִכָּל מְלַאכְתּוֹ אֲשֶׁר עָשָׂה:

And the Master of all strength Who is able to do anything blessed the seventh day with additional good

וַיְבָרֶךְ אֱלֹהִים אֶת יוֹם הַשְּׁבִיעִי

and He commanded the *Yidden* to rest on it thereby making it holy

וַיְקַדֵּשׁ אֹתוֹ

because on it He abstained from all His work of creation

כִּי בוֹ שָׁבַת מִכָּל מְלַאכְתּוֹ

that the Master of all strength Who is able to do anything created in the six days of creation

אֲשֶׁר בָּרָא אֱלֹהִים

from doing (any more creating).

לַעֲשׂוֹת:

The Master of all strength Who is able to do anything and Who takes care of us with Divine Providence

אֱלֹהֵינוּ

and the God Who took care of our Fathers with Divine Providence

וֵאלֹהֵי אֲבוֹתֵינוּ

let our rest be pleasant before You;

רְצֵה בִמְנוּחָתֵנוּ

make us holy from Above so that we should keep Your *mitzvos* properly

קַדְּשֵׁנוּ בְּמִצְוֹתֶיךָ

and grant us Divine assistance that all of our occupation should be in Torah study

וְתֵן חֶלְקֵנוּ בְּתוֹרָתֶךָ

bestow upon us good in a way that we will be satisfied with what we have (and not pursue our desires)   שַׂבְּעֵנוּ מִטּוּבֶךְ

and cause us to rejoice through the salvation that You will bring us   וְשַׂמְּחֵנוּ בִּישׁוּעָתֶךְ

and (we ask that You) purify our hearts so that we serve You sincerely (without other motives)   וְטַהֵר לִבֵּנוּ לְעָבְדְּךָ בֶּאֱמֶת

and give us as an inheritance (the holiness that Shabbos inspires)   וְהַנְחִילֵנוּ

Master of all, the Master of all strength Who is able to do anything and Who takes care of us with Divine Providence   יהוה אֱלֹהֵינוּ

because of the love that You have for us (by giving us Shabbos)   בְּאַהֲבָה

and because of the desire You have for us (that You want us to bring sacrifices even on Shabbos)   וּבְרָצוֹן

[give us as an inheritance] (the inspiration of) Shabbos that You made holy   שַׁבַּת קָדְשֶׁךָ

and (through this inspiration) You should cause Israel to have a complete rest on Shabbos   וְיָנוּחוּ בָה [12] יִשְׂרָאֵל

for they sanctify Your Name (by keeping Shabbos)   מְקַדְּשֵׁי שְׁמֶךָ

You are the Source of Blessing, Master of all   בָּרוּךְ אַתָּה יהוה

Who made the Shabbos holier (than the other days — and gave it to us as a present).[13]   מְקַדֵּשׁ הַשַּׁבָּת.

---

12 *Mishnah Berurah* (268:1) cites the custom to say בָה in *Maariv* on Shabbos, בּוֹ in *Shacharis*, and בָם in *Minchah*. The reason for this is of *kabbalistic* origin (see footnote of *Siach Yitzchok* in *Siddur Ha'Gra*). Some have a custom to always say בָה which is grammatically more correct (*Avodas Yisrael*; see also *Kaf Hachayim* 268:2).

13. One should concentrate at this point on giving great praise and thanks to Hashem for this great gift of Shabbos, and he should give this thanks with great joy. (*Yesod Veshoresh Ha'avodah*)

עבודה
Return of the Temple Service

Be pleased[14]	רְצֵה
Master of all	יהוה
the Master of all strength, Who is able to do anything and Who takes care of us with Divine Providence	אֱלֹהֵינוּ
with Your nation, Israel (because they are praying for the rebuilding of the Temple)	בְּעַמְּךָ יִשְׂרָאֵל
and with their prayer (for the rebuilding of the Temple)[15]	וּבִתְפִלָּתָם
and return the service of the Temple	וְהָשֵׁב אֶת הָעֲבוֹדָה
(even) to the Holy of Holies.	לִדְבִיר בֵּיתֶךָ
And the fire-offerings that they will bring	וְאִשֵּׁי יִשְׂרָאֵל
and the prayer of Israel (which is now in place of the offerings)	וּתְפִלָּתָם
because of Your love for the Jews	בְּאַהֲבָה
accept with desire	תְקַבֵּל בְּרָצוֹן

---

14. Before this blessing one should instill in his heart the love of all Jews, no matter what country or group they belong to, for we ask God here that He should be pleased with all of His nation, Israel. [The saintly Chofetz Chaim wrote in *Ahavas Yisrael* (Ch. 2) that we pray constantly for the rebuilding of the Temple, but we don't contemplate the cause of its destruction, which was hatred for an unjustifiable reason. Therefore if we want the Temple to be rebuilt we first must rectify this sin and love all Jews.]

15. R' Yehuda ben Yakar (13th cent.) writes that because Jews pray in every *Shemoneh Esray* for the rebuilding of the Temple (and not just for material things, as gentiles do), God should accept and answer our prayers.

and help us that it should always be desirable

וּתְהִי לְרָצוֹן תָּמִיד

the service (whether offerings or prayers) of Israel, Your nation.

עֲבוֹדַת יִשְׂרָאֵל עַמֶּךָ

ON *ROSH CHODESH* AND ON *CHOL HAMOED* THE FOLLOWING IS SAID:

The Master of all strength Who is able to do anything and Who takes care of us with Divine Providence

אֱלֹהֵינוּ

and the God who took care of our Fathers with Divine Providence,

וֵאלֹהֵי אֲבוֹתֵינוּ

may our remembrance and consideration go up

יַעֲלֶה

and come

וְיָבֹא

and reach

וְיַגִּיעַ

and be seen in a good way

וְיֵרָאֶה

and be accepted with desire

וְיֵרָצֶה

and be heard well

וְיִשָּׁמַע

and be considered

וְיִפָּקֵד

and be remembered forever

וְיִזָּכֵר

our remembrance, i.e., our special relationship with You

זִכְרוֹנֵנוּ

and Your special consideration to do good for us

וּפִקְדוֹנֵנוּ

and the remembrance of the covenants You made with our Fathers

וְזִכְרוֹן אֲבוֹתֵינוּ

and the remembrance of the promise to bring *Mashiach*, a descendant of David Your servant

וְזִכְרוֹן מָשִׁיחַ בֶּן דָּוִד עַבְדֶּךָ

and the remembrance of Jerusalem, the city of Your Holiness, which is now in ruins

וְזִכְרוֹן יְרוּשָׁלַיִם עִיר קָדְשֶׁךָ

and the remembrance of Your nation, the House of Israel, which is now in exile

וְזִכְרוֹן כָּל עַמְּךָ בֵּית יִשְׂרָאֵל

(may all of these remembrances) come before You	לְפָנֶיךָ
for salvation (for all of Israel)	לִפְלֵיטָה
for good (for all of Israel)	לְטוֹבָה
to find favor in Your eyes and in everyone's eyes	לְחֵן
and to grant us our requests (even though we are not deserving)	וּלְחֶסֶד
and for mercy (not punishing us according to our wrongdoings)	וּלְרַחֲמִים
and for life (for all of Israel)	לְחַיִּים
and for peace (for all of Israel)	וּלְשָׁלוֹם

on this day of *Rosh Chodesh*	בְּיוֹם רֹאשׁ הַחֹדֶשׁ הַזֶּה	On *Rosh Chodesh*
on this day of the Festival of *Matzos*	בְּיוֹם חַג הַמַּצּוֹת הַזֶּה	On *Chol Hamoed Pesach*
on this day of the Festival of *Succos*	בְּיוֹם חַג הַסֻּכּוֹת הַזֶּה	On *Chol Hamoed Succos*

Remember us, Master of all	זָכְרֵנוּ יהוה
the Master of all strength, Who is able to do anything and Who takes care of us with Divine Providence	אֱלֹהֵינוּ
[remember us] on this day to give everyone whatever is good for him	בּוֹ לְטוֹבָה
and consider us on this day for prosperity and success	וּפָקְדֵנוּ בוֹ לִבְרָכָה
and save us on this day so that we will merit life.	וְהוֹשִׁיעֵנוּ בוֹ לְחַיִּים
And with Your promise to save us and to have mercy on us	וּבִדְבַר יְשׁוּעָה וְרַחֲמִים
have mercy on us because You are our Creator, and favor us (with salvation)	חוּס וְחָנֵּנוּ
and have mercy on us because of our lowly nature and save us, even though we are undeserving	וְרַחֵם עָלֵינוּ וְהוֹשִׁיעֵנוּ
because our eyes are looking to You in hope	כִּי אֵלֶיךָ עֵינֵינוּ
because You are the Almighty King over all	כִּי אֵל מֶלֶךְ
and You are gracious and merciful (even to the undeserving).	חַנּוּן וְרַחוּם אָתָּה.

And let us merit to see (the *Shechinah* — Divine Presence) with our own eyes (i.e., soon, in our days)	וְתֶחֱזֶינָה עֵינֵינוּ
when You return Your Presence to the Temple (even if it is) in mercy (and not through our merits)	בְּשׁוּבְךָ לְצִיּוֹן בְּרַחֲמִים
You are the Source of Blessing, Master of all	בָּרוּךְ אַתָּה יהוה
Who will return His Divine Presence to the Temple.	הַמַּחֲזִיר שְׁכִינָתוֹ לְצִיּוֹן.

הודאה
Thanking God[16]

We give thanks to You, acknowledging	**מוֹדִים** אֲנַחְנוּ לָךְ
that You are the Master of all	שָׁאַתָּה הוּא יהוה
the Master of all strength, Who is able to do anything and Who takes care of us with Divine Providence	אֱלֹהֵינוּ
and the God Who took care of our Fathers with Divine Providence	וֵאלֹהֵי אֲבוֹתֵינוּ
(and that You will continue to take care of us) forever	לְעוֹלָם וָעֶד
[You are] the Rock — Creator and Sustainer — of our lives	צוּר חַיֵּינוּ
[and You are] the Protector Who saves us from all troubles	מָגֵן יִשְׁעֵנוּ

---

16. The *Bais Elokim* explains that the reason we bow at the beginning and end of this *berachah* is to show humility, recognizing our unworthiness for *Hashem's* special care, and realizing that all our lives and all goodness come from Him.

You are the One [Who keeps us alive and saves us] in every generation.

אַתָּה הוּא לְדוֹר וָדוֹר

We will always express our thanks to You

נוֹדֶה לְּךָ

and we will tell Your praise to others

וּנְסַפֵּר תְּהִלָּתֶךָ

for our lives — each breath — that is given over into Your hand

עַל חַיֵּינוּ הַמְּסוּרִים בְּיָדֶךָ

and for our souls that are entrusted to You (while we sleep) [17]

וְעַל נִשְׁמוֹתֵינוּ הַפְּקוּדוֹת לָךְ

and for the hidden miracles that You do for us every day [18]

וְעַל נִסֶּיךָ שֶׁבְּכָל יוֹם עִמָּנוּ

and for Your wonders of "nature" (which You renew constantly) [19]

וְעַל נִפְלְאוֹתֶיךָ

and for Your favors (that You do for us constantly)

וְטוֹבוֹתֶיךָ

---

17. The *Midrash* (*Tehillim* 25) tells us that every night a person gives over his weary soul to God, and He returns it each morning renewed. It is concerning this that we say the *berachah* of "*Elokai Neshamah*" each morning.

18. R' Bachai [R' Bachai ben Asher (14th cent.)] writes in his introduction to *Parshas Ki Sisa,* **"There isn't any individual in Israel** (*Klal Yisrael*) **for whom hidden miracles don't happen** *every day!***"**

19. The wonders of nature that have been revealed by mankind so far are far too numerous for anyone to think about. But if one would think about one of the myriad wonders while saying this prayer, the words would be so much more meaningful. The *Chovos Halevovos* [R' Bachai ibn Pakuda (11th cent.)] (*Shaar HaBechinah*, ch. 5) writes that the wonders in one's own body are the closest to him and are the ones he should ponder.

   To cite just one example: Hashem made two ears on every person in a way that they gather the most sounds. They are so sensitive that they can pick up a whisper from the other end of a room. There are really three sections to the ear: first, the outer ear that ends with the ear drum, which vibrates according to the loudness of the sound striking it, and sets off a chain reaction of events that causes us to recognize and understand the noise we hear, even though the vibration is just **one-billionth of a centimeter!** Behind the eardrum is the middle ear, which consists of three tiny bones that amplify the vibrations of the eardrum until they are

that You do in all parts of the day

שֶׁבְּכָל עֵת

in the evening, morning, and afternoon.

עֶרֶב וָבֹקֶר וְצָהֳרָיִם

You are the ultimate Good One

הַטּוֹב

for Your mercy has never finished — for You withhold punishment from those deserving it

כִּי לֹא כָלוּ רַחֲמֶיךָ

and You are the ultimate Merciful One (Who not only withholds punishment, but...)

וְהַמְרַחֵם

Whose kindness never ends — for You even give these undeserving people additional kindnesses

כִּי לֹא תַמּוּ חֲסָדֶיךָ

we have always put our hope in You.

מֵעוֹלָם קִוִּינוּ לָךְ

On Chanukah and Purim one adds עַל הַנִּסִים found on p. 90.

And for all of these wonders and favors that You do for us constantly

וְעַל כֻּלָּם

[Your Name] should be praised with the recognition that You are the Source of all Blessing

יִתְבָּרַךְ

and may Your Name (which represents Your acts) be exalted through the recognition of Your greatness

וְיִתְרוֹמַם שִׁמְךָ

---

approximately thirty times stronger. These vibrations then enter the amazingly complex inner ear. The inner ear's main component is a fluid-filled coil (called the cochlea) whose twisted interior is studded with about 20,000 tiny hairs that move in the fluid according to the vibrations that pass through it — each hair reacting to a different sound! This waving causes a tiny wisp of electricity that feeds into the auditory nerve (which is the thickness of a pencil lead and contains more than 30,000 electrical circuits). In all, thousands of different messages pour simultaneously into the brain, which then unscrambles the flood of data and hands down the verdict of what you heard — and all this in a split second! And it is another wonder that the brain can decipher all the different noises that one hears at one time (such as a person talking to you, someone knocking at the door, and the phone ringing simultaneously) as well as tell you from where these sounds are coming. (*Designer World*, Rabbi Avrohom Katz, p. 23-26; *Bais Yechezkel*, Rabbi Moshe Yechiel Weiss, *Hilchos Daios*, p. 98).

since You are our King (Who takes care of us especially) [we desire that Your Name be praised and exalted]

מַלְכֵּנוּ

constantly, every day

תָּמִיד

forever and ever.

לְעוֹלָם וָעֶד.

ON SHABBOS SHUVAH THE FOLLOWING IS ADDED:

And inscribe for a good life (i.e., life that will be good for earning the World to Come)

וּכְתוֹב לְחַיִּים טוֹבִים

all the children of Your covenant

כָּל בְּנֵי בְרִיתֶךָ

And all the living (those who will come back to life by the Revival of the Dead)

וְכֹל הַחַיִּים

will thank You constantly forever

יוֹדוּךָ סֶּלָה

and they will praise Your Name (which comes from Your deeds) truthfully, without any other motive

וִיהַלְלוּ אֶת שִׁמְךָ בֶּאֱמֶת

the Almighty

הָאֵל

Who saves us in all our troubles

יְשׁוּעָתֵנוּ

and Who helps us to succeed

וְעֶזְרָתֵנוּ

constantly, forever

סֶלָה

You are the Source of Blessing, Master of all

בָּרוּךְ אַתָּה יהוה

Whose Name is "The Good One" (for You are the ultimate good)

הַטּוֹב שִׁמְךָ

and to You alone is it fitting to give thanks (because You are the cause of all goodness).

וּלְךָ נָאֶה לְהוֹדוֹת.

שָׁלוֹם
Peace[20]

An abundant peace (which includes peace of mind, peace in one's house, peace between Jews, and peace in one's country)	שָׁלוֹם רָב
May You place upon Israel, Your nation, forever	עַל יִשְׂרָאֵל עַמְּךָ תָּשִׂים לְעוֹלָם
for You are the King over all	כִּי אַתָּה הוּא מֶלֶךְ
(and) the Master of all forms of peace (You can make peace in any situation).	אָדוֹן לְכָל הַשָּׁלוֹם
And it should be good in Your eyes	וְטוֹב בְּעֵינֶיךָ
to give an abundance of goodness and success to Your nation, Israel	לְבָרֵךְ אֶת עַמְּךָ יִשְׂרָאֵל
in all parts of the day	בְּכָל עֵת
and in all hours of each part of the day	וּבְכָל שָׁעָה
with Your peace (which is a complete peace).	בִּשְׁלוֹמֶךָ.

ON SHABBOS SHUVAH THE FOLLOWING IS ADDED:

In the book of life (of ...)	בְּסֵפֶר חַיִּים
of abundant goodness and success	בְּרָכָה
and peace between a man and his friend	וְשָׁלוֹם

---

20. The last *mishnah* states that God found no adequate vehicle for Israel's blessing other than peace. The Sages tell us (*Vayikra Rabbah* 9:9) that peace is so great that it comes at the end of all prayers. As the *Seder Hayom* [R' Moshe ben Yehuda Machir (16th cent.)] writes, "Peace encompasses everything and through peace we will merit everything." Therefore, one should concentrate especially on this all-encompassing final *berachah*.

and a good (ample and easy) livelihood	וּפַרְנָסָה טוֹבָה
may we be remembered	נִזָּכֵר
and may we be inscribed before You	וְנִכָּתֵב לְפָנֶיךָ
we (who are standing together praying)	אֲנַחְנוּ
and all of Your nation, Israel	וְכָל עַמְּךָ בֵּית יִשְׂרָאֵל
(let us be remembered and inscribed) for a truly good life (i.e., a life that will enable us to earn the World to Come)	לְחַיִּים טוֹבִים
and for peace within ourselves (that we should be satisfied with the materialistic things that we have)	וּלְשָׁלוֹם

SOME SAY THE FOLLOWING CONCLUSION ON SHABBOS SHUVAH
INSTEAD OF THE REGULAR CONCLUSION TO THE BLESSING

(You are the Source of Blessing, Master of all	(בָּרוּךְ אַתָּה יהוה
Who makes peace among all.)	עוֹשֶׂה הַשָּׁלוֹם.)

You are the Source of Blessing, Master of all   **בָּרוּךְ אַתָּה יהוה**

Who gives an abundance of goodness and success to His nation, Israel, with peace.   **הַמְבָרֵךְ אֶת עַמּוֹ יִשְׂרָאֵל בַּשָּׁלוֹם.**

תחנונים
Personal Requests [21]

The Master of all strength Who is able to do anything and Who takes care of me with Divine Providence   **אֱלֹהַי**

help me to guard my tongue from speaking bad about others (*Lashon Hora*)   **נְצוֹר לְשׁוֹנִי מֵרָע**

---

21. Concerning the asking of additional personal requests on Shabbos: it is mentioned several times in *Mishnah Berurah* (see ibid. 188:9, 288:22, 294:2 and 584:4) that it is prohibited. The *Rambam* (*Pe'er Hador* 30) was asked specifically about this and in his responsa he wrote the following: "These [additional] requests and prayers that they have copied from the works of the *Geonim,* I do not think that it is proper to say them, not an individual and not the congregation, not on Shabbos and not on *Yom Tov* ... for one should only mention on Shabbos and *Yom Tov* things that are pleasant and make one happy, and to mention the wonders that Hashem did with our forefathers and us." See *Oz Nidberu* (14:23), who, after citing this *Rambam,*

and [help me to guard] my lips from speaking deceit or falsehood

וּשְׂפָתַי מִדַּבֵּר מִרְמָה

and help me so that my soul should be silent (that even in thought I should not get angry) at those who curse me

וְלִמְקַלְלַי נַפְשִׁי תִדֹּם

and help me so that my soul should be like dust (very humble) before everyone (and not mind insults).

וְנַפְשִׁי כֶּעָפָר לַכֹּל תִּהְיֶה

Open up my heart so that it should be receptive and understand Your Torah

פְּתַח לִבִּי בְּתוֹרָתֶךָ

and help my soul eagerly pursue Your *mitzvos*

וּבְמִצְוֹתֶיךָ תִּרְדּוֹף נַפְשִׁי

and all those who want to harm me (whether in mundane matters or spiritual matters, i.e., to cause me to sin)

וְכֹל הַחוֹשְׁבִים עָלַי רָעָה

quickly annul their plan

מְהֵרָה הָפֵר עֲצָתָם

and ruin their thought (even before they make plans).

וְקַלְקֵל מַחֲשַׁבְתָּם

Act (take us out of exile) for the sake of Your Name, which is desecrated now among the gentiles [22]

עֲשֵׂה לְמַעַן שְׁמֶךָ

act (take us out of exile) for the sake of Your right hand, [23] which You have now withdrawn in our exile

עֲשֵׂה לְמַעַן יְמִינֶךָ

---

rules that one should be stringent not to request anything, neither spiritual nor material, except that which the entire congregation usually says [e.g. אֱלֹהַי נְצוֹר].

22. The *Tur* [R' Yaakov ben Asher (1270 - 1343)] wrote (*Orach Chayim*, ch. 122) that anyone who is careful to say these four phrases (starting with this one) will merit to greet the Divine Presence. At the end of our prayers we reiterate that which is most important to us — the honor of God — and therefore we ask God to take us out of the exile for His sake, for the whole world to see His glory. One who says this sincerely will merit greeting the Divine Presence.

23. The "right hand" of God symbolizes His redeeming power (*The World of Prayer*).

act (take us out of exile) for the sake of Your Holiness (so that all will know that You lead us with holiness)	עֲשֵׂה לְמַעַן קְדֻשָּׁתֶךָ
act (take us out of exile) for the sake of Your Torah (so the Torah can be studied properly and completely)	עֲשֵׂה לְמַעַן תּוֹרָתֶךָ
and in order that Your dear ones, Israel, should be released from all troubles	לְמַעַן יֵחָלְצוּן יְדִידֶיךָ
save them with (the wonders and miracles that are attributed to) Your right hand	הוֹשִׁיעָה יְמִינְךָ
and answer (even) me in this prayer.	וַעֲנֵנִי.
Let the words of my prayer be desirable to You[24]	יִהְיוּ לְרָצוֹן אִמְרֵי פִי
and also the thoughts of my heart which I cannot express [should be desirable] before You	וְהֶגְיוֹן לִבִּי לְפָנֶיךָ
Master of all	יהוה
My Rock, Whom I rely on for all my requests	צוּרִי
and Who will be my Redeemer.	וְגוֹאֲלִי.

ONE SHOULD BOW AND GO BACK 3 STEPS LIKE A SERVANT DEPARTING FROM HIS MASTER

The One Who makes peace in Heaven (among the angels)	**עֹשֶׂה שָׁלוֹם** בִּמְרוֹמָיו
may He make peace (for those on earth, who are naturally quarrelsome)	הוּא יַעֲשֶׂה שָׁלוֹם
on those of us here (praying together)	עָלֵינוּ

---

24. *Seder Hayom* (quoted also in *Mishnah Brurah* 122:8) writes that one should say this verse with great concentration, for it will help a great deal that his prayers should not go unanswered.

and on all of Israel	וְעַל כָּל יִשְׂרָאֵל
and (you, the angels who escort me,) agree to my prayer, and say Amen!	וְאִמְרוּ אָמֵן.
May it be Your desire	**יְהִי רָצוֹן** מִלְּפָנֶיךָ
Master of all	יהוה
the Master of all strength, Who is able to do anything and Who takes care of us with Divine Providence	אֱלֹהֵינוּ
and the God Who took care of our Fathers with Divine Providence	וֵאלֹהֵי אֲבוֹתֵינוּ
that You should rebuild the Temple (so that we will be able to do the ultimate *avodah* - service to You)	שֶׁיִּבָּנֶה בֵּית הַמִּקְדָּשׁ
quickly and in our lifetime	בִּמְהֵרָה בְיָמֵינוּ
and help us so that all our toil should be in learning Your Torah.	וְתֵן חֶלְקֵנוּ בְּתוֹרָתֶךָ.
And there, in the Temple, we will bring offerings (the ultimate service) with reverence	וְשָׁם נַעֲבָדְךָ בְּיִרְאָה
as [they brought offerings and served in reverence] in the earlier days (of Moshe)	כִּימֵי עוֹלָם
and as they did in the previous years (of Shlomo Hamelech).	וּכְשָׁנִים קַדְמוֹנִיּוֹת.
And then, it will be pleasing to the Master of all	וְעָרְבָה לַיהוה
the offerings that will be brought in the Temple (which is in the portion of Yehudah in Jerusalem)	מִנְחַת יְהוּדָה וִירוּשָׁלָיִם
as [the offerings were pleasing] in the earlier days (of Moshe)	כִּימֵי עוֹלָם
and as they were in the previous years (of Shlomo Hamelech).	וּכְשָׁנִים קַדְמוֹנִיּוֹת.

שחרית לשבת
Shacharis for Shabbos

Master of all — in particular, My Master   אֲדֹנָי

please open my lips (because I am afraid and ashamed to open them)   שְׂפָתַי תִּפְתָּח

and [help me pray with concentration, so] my mouth will [be able to] tell Your true praise   וּפִי יַגִּיד תְּהִלָּתֶךָ.

אבות
Our God and the God of Our Fathers, Who Created Everything, and Protected Abraham[1]

You are the source of blessing (an expression of praise)   **בָּרוּךְ** אַתָּה

Master of all (Who always was, is, and will be)   יהוה

the Master of all strength Who is able to do anything and Who takes care of us with Divine Providence   אֱלֹהֵינוּ

and the God Who took care of our Fathers with Divine Providence (and made a covenant with each of them)   וֵאלֹהֵי אֲבוֹתֵינוּ

the God Who made a covenant with our father Abraham (who excelled in kindness)   אֱלֹהֵי אַבְרָהָם

the God Who made a covenant with our father Isaac (who excelled in service of God)   אֱלֹהֵי יִצְחָק

---

1. One must be very careful to concentrate when saying this *berachah*, because otherwise he does not fulfill his obligation to pray. In the time of the *Gemarah* one would have to repeat the *Shemoneh Esray* if he had not concentrated on it. Nowadays, however, when we are not sure that the second time will yield the proper concentration either, we do not repeat the *Shemoneh Esray*. However, the *Mishnah Berurah* [the authoritative *halachic* work] (101:4) states that if one did not yet say ברוך אתה ה׳ at the end of this *berachah*, he can go back to אלהי אברהם and repeat from there with concentration, thereby rectifying his previous lack of concentration.

and the God Who made a covenant with our father Jacob (who excelled in learning Torah)	וֵאלֹהֵי יַעֲקֹב
He is the Almighty (all power is His, especially in exercising the attribute of mercy)	הָאֵל
Who is the Great One (all greatness is His, especially in exercising the attribute of kindness)	הַגָּדוֹל
(and) He is the Strong One (all strength is His, especially in exercising the attribute of judgment)	הַגִּבּוֹר
and He alone deserves to be feared (because no being has the ability to do good or bad except Him)	וְהַנּוֹרָא
for He is the supreme God Who is the ultimate cause of everything	אֵל עֶלְיוֹן
Who always does kindnesses that are purely good	גּוֹמֵל חֲסָדִים טוֹבִים
and He recreates everything, constantly, every day	וְקוֹנֵה הַכֹּל
and every day He recalls for our benefit the kindnesses performed by the forefathers	וְזוֹכֵר חַסְדֵי אָבוֹת
and He constantly brings the Redeemer closer	וּמֵבִיא גוֹאֵל
to the forefathers' childrens' children (even though the merit of the forefathers might already be used up)	לִבְנֵי בְנֵיהֶם
for the sake of His Name (which will be sanctified at the time of the Redemption)	לְמַעַן שְׁמוֹ
[and He will also bring the Redeemer] because of His great love for the Jewish people	בְּאַהֲבָה

Remember us for life in this world (in order that we may earn the World to Come by doing *mitzvos* here)	זָכְרֵנוּ לְחַיִּים

King, Who desires life (and not death for a sinner, but rather that he should repent)	מֶלֶךְ חָפֵץ בַּחַיִּים
and write us in the Book of the Righteous, for life	וְכָתְבֵנוּ בְּסֵפֶר הַחַיִּים
for Your sake, in order that we may serve You	לְמַעַנְךָ
the Master of all strength Who is able to do anything and is the One Who apportions life to all	אֱלֹהִים חַיִּים

He is the King over all	מֶלֶךְ
Who is the Helper (to help one succeed)	עוֹזֵר
and the Savior (from trouble)	וּמוֹשִׁיעַ
and the Protector (to prevent trouble from coming)	וּמָגֵן
You are the Source of Blessing, Master of all	בָּרוּךְ אַתָּה יהוה
the Protector of Abraham (and because of Abraham He continues His protection over us).	מָגֵן אַבְרָהָם:

<h1 style="text-align:center">גבורות</h1>

The Mighty Acts of God and the Revival of the Dead

You alone are eternally Strong	**אַתָּה** גִּבּוֹר לְעוֹלָם
Master of all	אֲדֹנָי
You even revive the dead (which shows the greatest strength, contradicting all laws of nature)	מְחַיֵּה מֵתִים אַתָּה
[and] You have an abundance of strength with which to save	רַב לְהוֹשִׁיעַ

FROM *MUSAF* OF *SHEMINI ATSERES* UNTIL AFTER *MUSAF* OF THE FIRST DAY OF *PESACH*, SAY:

He causes the wind to blow (which aids evaporation, blows clouds where they are needed, and facilitates all aspects of rain)	מַשִּׁיב הָרִוּחַ
and He causes every drop of rain to fall on its desired place (and for its designated function: to nourish or to flood, etc.)	וּמוֹרִיד הַגֶּשֶׁם

He provides all the living with their food and other needs in kindness (not because they are deserving)   מְכַלְכֵּל חַיִּים בְּחֶסֶד

He revives the dead with great mercy (searching for merits with which they would deserve revival)   מְחַיֶּה מֵתִים בְּרַחֲמִים רַבִּים

He supports those who are falling (whether physically, emotionally, or financially)   סוֹמֵךְ נוֹפְלִים

and He heals the sick from all types of illnesses (even when doctors have given up hope)   וְרוֹפֵא חוֹלִים

and He opens the bonds of those who are restricted (e.g., giving movement to our limbs when we awaken)   וּמַתִּיר אֲסוּרִים

and He will keep His promise to those sleeping in the dust (the dead), to revive them.   וּמְקַיֵּם אֱמוּנָתוֹ לִישֵׁנֵי עָפָר

Who is like You (who can do as many mighty deeds, which are infinite, even for one person)?   מִי כָמוֹךָ

— You, to Whom all mighty deeds belong! —   בַּעַל גְּבוּרוֹת

And who is comparable to You in even one of Your mighty deeds (which are of the highest quality)?   וּמִי דוֹמֶה לָּךְ

You are the King over all   מֶלֶךְ

Who causes death and revival in many respects (such as sleep and awakening, poverty and wealth)   מֵמִית וּמְחַיֶּה

and, like the sprouting of a seed, You bring the Salvation (the Revival of the Dead)   וּמַצְמִיחַ יְשׁוּעָה

Who is like You, who has as much mercy on his sons as You, the Merciful Father, have for us	מִי כָמוֹךָ אַב הָרַחֲמִים
(and) remembers His creatures, out of mercy, for life	זוֹכֵר יְצוּרָיו לְחַיִּים בְּרַחֲמִים
And (from the mighty deeds that we mentioned) we see that You are surely trusted to revive the dead	וְנֶאֱמָן אַתָּה לְהַחֲיוֹת מֵתִים
You are the Source of Blessing, Master of all	בָּרוּךְ אַתָּה יהוה
the Reviver of all the dead (from Adam until the time of the Revival). 2	מְחַיֵּה הַמֵּתִים :

קדושת השם
Holiness of God

You, Yourself, are holy (different and separate from everything)	**אַתָּה** קָדוֹשׁ
and Your Name (which comes from Your many acts) reveals holiness	וְשִׁמְךָ קָדוֹשׁ
and the holy ones — Israel	וּקְדוֹשִׁים
constantly praise You, every day, forever	בְּכָל יוֹם יְהַלְלוּךָ סֶּלָה
You are the Source of Blessing, Master of all	בָּרוּךְ אַתָּה יהוה
the Almighty, Who is holier than all else.	הָאֵל הַקָּדוֹשׁ.

the King Who is holier than all else.	הַמֶּלֶךְ הַקָּדוֹשׁ.

---

2. Even though many bodies have decomposed over thousands of years, and some have been burned and their dust has been scattered, and others have drowned at sea, *Hashem* with His great might will recognize and recompose the bodies and return to them their original souls (*Yesod Veshoresh Ha'avodah*).

קְדוּשַׁת הַיּוֹם - שַׁבָּת מַתַּן תּוֹרָה
Holiness of the Day - The Shabbos of the Giving of the Torah[3]

Moshe[4] should rejoice (in the world of souls [where he is presently])	**יִשְׂמַח** מֹשֶׁה
because of the great present of the Torah that was given through him	בְּמַתְּנַת חֶלְקוֹ
for Hashem called him a faithful servant (therefore he merited the Torah)	כִּי עֶבֶד נֶאֱמָן קָרָאתָ לּוֹ
You gave him a crown of glory on his head — the shine on his face[5]	כְּלִיל תִּפְאֶרֶת בְּרֹאשׁוֹ נָתַתָּ (לּוֹ)
when he stood before You on Mount Sinai (to receive the second tablets)	בְּעׇמְדוֹ לְפָנֶיךָ עַל הַר סִינָי
and the two tablets of stone he brought down with his hand	וּשְׁנֵי לוּחוֹת אֲבָנִים הוֹרִיד בְּיָדוֹ
and it was written on the (second) tablets the "observance of Shabbos"	וְכָתוּב בָּהֶם שְׁמִירַת שַׁבָּת
and so it is written in Your Torah (besides on the tablets) about keeping Shabbos, to show how important it is. And so it states (*Shemos* 31:16):	וְכֵן כָּתוּב בְּתוֹרָתֶךָ:

---

3. *Avudraham* says that some early commentators asked why the Sages instituted three different prayers for *Maariv, Shacharis and Minchah* of Shabbos, whereas on Yom Tov they instituted one prayer for all three. He quotes an answer in the name of R' Kalonymus (and the *Tur* [O.C. 292] writes likewise), that the three prayers of Shabbos represent three different "Shabbosos": *Maariv* corresponds to the Shabbos of Creation; *Shacharis* corresponds to the Shabbos on which the Torah was given; and *Mincha* corresponds to the Shabbos of the World to come.

4. *Shibolay Haleket* [R' Tzidkiyahu ben R' Avraham] (Ch. 76) asks, for what reason did the Sages mention Moshe's name here in the *tefillah*? He quotes R' Nosson ben Machir (11th cent.) who says that since the Torah was given through Moshe on Shabbos morning, therefore it is proper to mention his honor, for the Torah was given to him as a present.

5. See *Shemos* 34:29-35 that when Moshe came down from Mount Sinai with the second set of Tablets his face shined with a Divine radiance.

And the children of Israel should be careful to keep the Shabbos (by not doing any forbidden work)	וְשָׁמְרוּ בְנֵי יִשְׂרָאֵל אֶת הַשַּׁבָּת
(and) to make all the necessary preparations for the Shabbos (before Shabbos)	לַעֲשׂוֹת אֶת הַשַּׁבָּת
for their many generations	לְדֹרֹתָם
(and this will be) an eternal covenant.	בְּרִית עוֹלָם.
Between Me and between the children of Israel	בֵּינִי וּבֵין בְּנֵי יִשְׂרָאֵל
it is a sign forever (if you rest on Shabbos like He did)	אוֹת הִיא לְעֹלָם
that in six days	כִּי שֵׁשֶׁת יָמִים
the Master of all created	עָשָׂה יהוה
the heavens and the earth and all that was in them	אֶת הַשָּׁמַיִם וְאֶת הָאָרֶץ
and on the seventh day (Shabbos) He ceased from working	וּבַיּוֹם הַשְּׁבִיעִי שָׁבַת
and rested (even from saying anything).	וַיִּנָּפַשׁ.

And You, the Master of all, the Master of all strength Who is able to do anything and Who takes care of us with Divine Providence did not give Shabbos as a day of rest[6] **וְלֹא נְתַתּוֹ** יהוה אֱלֹהֵינוּ

---

6. Citing this phrase of the prayer, *Malbim* [R' Meir Leibush Malbim (1809-1879)] (*Shemos* 31:17) writes that Hashem promised that the gentiles will not accept Shabbos as their day of rest [as we know, the gentiles rest either on Friday or Sunday]. See *Ya'aros D'vash* [R' Yonasan Eybschuetz (1690-1764)] (II:3) who also mentions this passage, and writes that Hashem caused even those nations that had originally kept the seventh day, to adopt a different day of rest.

to the nations of the lands (that think their land is the most important thing, and don't believe at all in Hashem)   לְגוֹיֵי הָאֲרָצוֹת

and You, our King, did not give the Shabbos as an inheritance   וְלֹא הִנְחַלְתּוֹ מַלְכֵּנוּ

to idol worshipers   לְעוֹבְדֵי פְסִילִים

and also, in the rest of Shabbos   וְגַם בִּמְנוּחָתוֹ

(even) the gentiles (who accept not to worship idols) will not dwell for they are uncircumcised   לֹא יִשְׁכְּנוּ עֲרֵלִים

but to Israel (who accepted all Your *mitzvos* and are therefore) Your nation   כִּי לְיִשְׂרָאֵל עַמְּךָ

with love You gave Shabbos, which is the best gift[7]   נְתַתּוֹ בְּאַהֲבָה

specifically to the descendants of Jacob, whom You have chosen.[8]   לְזֶרַע יַעֲקֹב אֲשֶׁר בָּם בָּחָרְתָּ

The nation (Israel) who makes the seventh day (Shabbos) holy (by not working on it)   עַם מְקַדְּשֵׁי שְׁבִיעִי

they will all be satisfied and still delight from Your spiritual good (in the future)   כֻּלָּם יִשְׂבְּעוּ וְיִתְעַנְּגוּ מִטּוּבֶךָ

for in the seventh day You were pleased and made it holy (to be a day of rest from work)   וּבַשְּׁבִיעִי רָצִיתָ בּוֹ וְקִדַּשְׁתּוֹ

(and) to be the most desirable day of the week   חֶמְדַּת יָמִים

(and) You called it "Shabbos"   אוֹתוֹ קָרָאתָ

as a remembrance to the work of creation (that He ceased from work on the seventh day).   זֵכֶר לְמַעֲשֵׂה בְרֵאשִׁית.

---

7. One should think here to give a tremendous thanks to Hashem for the great gift of Shabbos. (*Nehorah Hasholeim*)

8. One should concentrate here on giving a tremendous thanks to Hashem for putting his portion amongst the holy nation of Israel, that He has chosen. (*ibid.*)

The Master of all strength Who is able to do anything and Who takes care of us with Divine Providence אֱלֹהֵינוּ

and the God Who took care of our Fathers with Divine Providence וֵאלֹהֵי אֲבוֹתֵינוּ

let our rest be pleasant before You; רְצֵה בִמְנוּחָתֵנוּ

make us holy from Above so that we should keep Your mitzvos properly קַדְּשֵׁנוּ בְּמִצְוֹתֶיךָ

and grant us Divine assistance that all of our occupation should be in Torah study וְתֵן חֶלְקֵנוּ בְּתוֹרָתֶךָ

bestow upon us good in a way that we will be satisfied with what we have (and not pursue our desires) שַׂבְּעֵנוּ מִטּוּבֶךָ

and cause us to rejoice through the salvation that You will bring us וְשַׂמְּחֵנוּ בִּישׁוּעָתֶךָ

and (we ask that You) purify our hearts so that we serve You sincerely (without other motives) וְטַהֵר לִבֵּנוּ לְעָבְדְּךָ בֶּאֱמֶת

and give us as an inheritance (the holiness that Shabbos inspires) וְהַנְחִילֵנוּ

Master of all, the Master of all strength Who is able to do anything and Who takes care of us with Divine Providence יהוה אֱלֹהֵינוּ

because of the love that You have for us (by giving us Shabbos) בְּאַהֲבָה

and because of the desire You have for us (that You want us to bring sacrifices even on Shabbos) וּבְרָצוֹן

[give us as an inheritance] (the inspiration of) Shabbos that You made holy שַׁבַּת קָדְשֶׁךָ

and (through this inspiration) You should cause Israel to have a complete rest on Shabbos וְיָנוּחוּ בִי יִשְׂרָאֵל

for they sanctify Your Name (by keeping Shabbos) מְקַדְּשֵׁי שְׁמֶךָ

You are the Source of Blessing, Master of all	בָּרוּךְ אַתָּה יהוה
Who made the Shabbos holier (than the other days — and gave it to us as a present).[9]	מְקַדֵּשׁ הַשַּׁבָּת.

עבודה
Return of the Temple Service

Be pleased[10]	רְצֵה
Master of all	יהוה
the Master of all strength, Who is able to do anything and Who takes care of us with Divine Providence	אֱלֹהֵינוּ
with Your nation, Israel (because they are praying for the rebuilding of the Temple)	בְּעַמְּךָ יִשְׂרָאֵל
and with their prayer (for the rebuilding of the Temple)	וּבִתְפִלָּתָם
and return the service of the Temple	וְהָשֵׁב אֶת הָעֲבוֹדָה
(even) to the Holy of Holies.	לִדְבִיר בֵּיתֶךָ
And the fire-offerings that they will bring	וְאִשֵּׁי יִשְׂרָאֵל

---

9. One should concentrate at this point on giving great praise and thanks to Hashem for this great gift of Shabbos, and he should give this thanks with great joy. (*Yesod Veshoresh Ha'avodah*)

10. Before this blessing one should instill in his heart love of all Jews, no matter what country or group they belong to, for we ask God here that He should be pleased with all of His nation, Israel (*Darchay Chayim*) [The saintly Chofetz Chaim wrote in *Ahavas Yisrael* (Ch. 2) that we pray constantly for the rebuilding of the Temple, but we don't contemplate the cause of its destruction, which was hatred for an unjustifiable reason. Therefore if we want the Temple to be rebuilt we first must rectify this sin and love all Jews.]

and the prayer of Israel (which is now in place of the offerings)

וּתְפִלָּתָם

because of Your love for the Jews

בְּאַהֲבָה

accept with desire

תְקַבֵּל בְּרָצוֹן

and help us that it should always be desirable

וּתְהִי לְרָצוֹן תָּמִיד

the service (whether offerings or prayers) of Israel, Your nation

עֲבוֹדַת יִשְׂרָאֵל עַמֶּךָ

ON *ROSH CHODESH* AND ON *CHOL HAMOED* THE FOLLOWING IS SAID:

The Master of all strength Who is able to do anything and Who takes care of us with Divine Providence

אֱלֹהֵינוּ

and the God who took care of our Fathers with Divine Providence,

וֵאלֹהֵי אֲבוֹתֵינוּ

may our remembrance and consideration go up

יַעֲלֶה

and come

וְיָבֹא

and reach

וְיַגִּיעַ

and be seen in a good way

וְיֵרָאֶה

and be accepted with desire

וְיֵרָצֶה

and be heard well

וְיִשָּׁמַע

and be considered

וְיִפָּקֵד

and be remembered forever

וְיִזָּכֵר

our remembrance, i.e., our special relationship with You

זִכְרוֹנֵנוּ

and Your special consideration to do good for us

וּפִקְדוֹנֵנוּ

and the remembrance of the covenants You made with our Fathers	וְזִכְרוֹן אֲבוֹתֵינוּ
and the remembrance of the promise to bring *Mashiach*, a descendant of David Your servant	וְזִכְרוֹן מָשִׁיחַ בֶּן דָּוִד עַבְדֶּךָ
and the remembrance of Jerusalem, the city of Your Holiness, which is now in ruins	וְזִכְרוֹן יְרוּשָׁלַיִם עִיר קָדְשֶׁךָ
and the remembrance of Your nation, the House of Israel, which is now in exile	וְזִכְרוֹן כָּל עַמְּךָ בֵּית יִשְׂרָאֵל
(may all of these remembrances) come before You	לְפָנֶיךָ
for salvation (for all of Israel)	לִפְלֵיטָה
for good (for all of Israel)	לְטוֹבָה
to find favor in Your eyes and in everyone's eyes	לְחֵן
and to grant us our requests (even though we are not deserving)	וּלְחֶסֶד
and for mercy (not punishing us according to our wrongdoings)	וּלְרַחֲמִים
and for life (for all of Israel)	לְחַיִּים
and for peace (for all of Israel)	וּלְשָׁלוֹם

on this day of *Rosh Chodesh*	בְּיוֹם רֹאשׁ הַחֹדֶשׁ הַזֶּה	On *Rosh Chodesh*
on this day of the Festival of *Matzos*	בְּיוֹם חַג הַמַּצּוֹת הַזֶּה	On *Chol Hamoed Pesach*
on this day of the Festival of *Succos*	בְּיוֹם חַג הַסֻּכּוֹת הַזֶּה	On *Chol Hamoed Succos*

Remember us, Master of all	זָכְרֵנוּ יהוה
the Master of all strength, Who is able to do anything and Who takes care of us with Divine Providence	אֱלֹהֵינוּ
[remember us] on this day to give everyone whatever is good for him	בּוֹ לְטוֹבָה
and consider us on this day for prosperity and success	וּפָקְדֵנוּ בוֹ לִבְרָכָה
and save us on this day so that we will merit life	וְהוֹשִׁיעֵנוּ בוֹ לְחַיִּים
and with Your promise to save us and to have mercy on us	וּבִדְבַר יְשׁוּעָה וְרַחֲמִים

have mercy on us because You are our Creator, and favor us (with salvation)	חוּס וְחָנֵּנוּ
and have mercy on us because of our lowly nature and save us, even though we are undeserving	וְרַחֵם עָלֵינוּ וְהוֹשִׁיעֵנוּ
because our eyes are looking to You in hope	כִּי אֵלֶיךָ עֵינֵינוּ
because You are the Almighty King over all	כִּי אֵל מֶלֶךְ
and You are gracious and merciful (even to the undeserving).	חַנּוּן וְרַחוּם אָתָּה.

and let us merit to see (the *Shechinah* — Divine Presence) with our own eyes (i.e., soon, in our days)	וְתֶחֱזֶינָה עֵינֵינוּ
when You return Your Presence to the Temple (even if it is) in mercy (and not through our merits)	בְּשׁוּבְךָ לְצִיּוֹן בְּרַחֲמִים
You are the Source of Blessing, Master of all	בָּרוּךְ אַתָּה יהוה
Who will return His Divine Presence to the Temple.	הַמַּחֲזִיר שְׁכִינָתוֹ לְצִיּוֹן.

הודאה
Thanking God[11]

We give thanks to You, acknowledging	**מוֹדִים** אֲנַחְנוּ לָךְ
that You are the Master of all	שָׁאַתָּה הוּא יהוה
the Master of all strength, Who is able to do anything and Who takes care of us with Divine Providence	אֱלֹהֵינוּ
and the God Who took care of our Fathers with Divine Providence	וֵאלֹהֵי אֲבוֹתֵינוּ

---

11. The *Bais Elokim* explains that the reason we bow at the beginning and end of this *berachah* is to show humility, recognizing our unworthiness for *Hashem's* special care, and realizing that all our lives and all goodness come from Him.

(and that You will continue to take care of us) forever   לְעוֹלָם וָעֶד

[You are] the Rock — Creator and Sustainer — of our lives   צוּר חַיֵּינוּ

[and You are] the Protector Who saves us from all troubles   מָגֵן יִשְׁעֵנוּ

You are the One [Who keeps us alive and saves us] in every generation.   אַתָּה הוּא לְדוֹר וָדוֹר

We will always express our thanks to You   נוֹדֶה לְּךָ

and we will tell Your praise to others   וּנְסַפֵּר תְּהִלָּתֶךָ

for our lives — each breath — that is given over into Your hand   עַל חַיֵּינוּ הַמְּסוּרִים בְּיָדֶךָ

and for our souls that are entrusted to You (while we sleep)   וְעַל נִשְׁמוֹתֵינוּ הַפְּקוּדוֹת לָךְ

and for the hidden miracles that You do for us every day   וְעַל נִסֶּיךָ שֶׁבְּכָל יוֹם עִמָּנוּ

and for Your wonders of "nature" (which You renew constantly)   וְעַל נִפְלְאוֹתֶיךָ

and for Your favors (that You do for us constantly)   וְטוֹבוֹתֶיךָ

that You do in all parts of the day   שֶׁבְּכָל עֵת

in the evening, morning, and afternoon.   עֶרֶב וָבֹקֶר וְצָהֳרָיִם

You are the ultimate Good One   הַטּוֹב

for Your mercy has never finished   for You withhold punishment from those deserving it   כִּי לֹא כָלוּ רַחֲמֶיךָ

and You are the ultimate Merciful One (Who not only withholds punishment, but...)

וְהַמְרַחֵם

Whose kindness never ends — for You even give these undeserving people additional kindnesses

כִּי לֹא תַמּוּ חֲסָדֶיךָ

we have always put our hope in You.

מֵעוֹלָם קִוִּינוּ לָךְ

On Chanukah and Purim one adds עַל הַנִסִים found on p. 90.

And for all of these wonders and favors that You do for us constantly

וְעַל כֻּלָם

[Your Name] should be praised with the recognition that You are the Source of all Blessing

יִתְבָּרַךְ

and may Your Name (which represents Your acts) be exalted through the recognition of Your greatness

וְיִתְרוֹמַם שִׁמְךָ

since You are our King (Who takes care of us especially) [we desire that Your Name be praised and exalted]

מַלְכֵּנוּ

constantly, every day

תָּמִיד

forever and ever.

לְעוֹלָם וָעֶד.

On Shabbos Shuvah the following is added:

And inscribe for a good life (i.e., life that will be good for earning the World to Come)

וּכְתוֹב לְחַיִּים טוֹבִים

all the children of Your covenant

כָּל בְּנֵי בְרִיתֶךָ

And all the living (those who will come back to life by the Revival of the Dead)

וְכֹל הַחַיִּים

will thank You constantly forever

יוֹדוּךָ סֶּלָה

and they will praise Your Name (which comes from Your deeds) truthfully, without any other motive

וִיהַלְלוּ אֶת שִׁמְךָ בֶּאֱמֶת

the Almighty	הָאֵל

Who saves us in all our troubles   יְשׁוּעָתֵנוּ

and Who helps us to succeed   וְעֶזְרָתֵנוּ

constantly, forever   סֶלָה

You are the Source of Blessing, Master of all   בָּרוּךְ אַתָּה יהוה

Whose Name is "The Good One" (for You are the ultimate good)   הַטּוֹב שִׁמְךָ

and to You alone is it fitting to give thanks (because You are the cause of all goodness).   וּלְךָ נָאֶה לְהוֹדוֹת.

שלום
Peace[12]

Grant peace (which includes peace of mind, peace in one's house, peace between Jews, and peace in one's country)   שִׂים שָׁלוֹם

(and grant what is) good for each person   טוֹבָה

and (grant) prosperity and success   וּבְרָכָה

(and) let us find favor in Your eyes and thereby find favor in the eyes of all who see us   חֵן

and grant our requests (even though we are not deserving)   וָחֶסֶד

---

12. The last *mishnah* states that God found no adequate vehicle for Israel's blessing other than peace. The Sages tell us (*Vayikra Rabbah* 9:9) that peace is so great that it comes at the end of all prayers. As the *Seder Hayom* [R' Moshe ben Yehuda Machir (16th cent.)] writes, "Peace encompasses everything and through peace we will merit everything." Therefore, one should concentrate especially on this all-encompassing final *berachah*.

and have mercy on us (not to punish us according to our wrongdoings)	וְרַחֲמִים
on those of us here (praying together)	עָלֵינוּ
and on all of Israel, Your nation.	וְעַל כָּל יִשְׂרָאֵל עַמֶּךָ
Since You are our Father, give us an abundance of goodness and success	בָּרְכֵנוּ אָבִינוּ
all of us like one (equally)	כֻּלָּנוּ כְּאֶחָד
with the "light of Your face" (which is a symbol of Your great love)	בְּאוֹר פָּנֶיךָ
because, as we already know from the Revelation at Sinai, that with the "light of Your face" come great things:	כִּי בְאוֹר פָּנֶיךָ
You gave to us as a present (not because we were deserving),	נָתַתָּ לָּנוּ
Master of all	יהוה
the Master of all strength, Who is able to do anything and Who takes care of us with Divine Providence,	אֱלֹהֵינוּ
the Torah that teaches us how to live	תּוֹרַת חַיִּים
and (through it) the love of doing kindness	וְאַהֲבַת חֶסֶד
and (You gave us with the Torah more opportunities for) reward in the World to Come (by fulfilling the many *mitzvos*)	וּצְדָקָה
and (as reward for keeping the Torah You give us also) an abundance of goodness and success (in this world)	וּבְרָכָה
and (in the merit of keeping the Torah You give us) special mercy	וְרַחֲמִים

and (as a reward for keeping the Torah You give us) a long, healthy life   וְחַיִּים

and (through the Torah we have) peace of body and mind (because all the ways of the Torah are peaceful)   וְשָׁלוֹם

And it should be good in Your eyes   וְטוֹב בְּעֵינֶיךָ

to give an abundance of goodness and success to Your nation, Israel   לְבָרֵךְ אֶת עַמְּךָ יִשְׂרָאֵל

in all parts of the day   בְּכָל עֵת

and in all hours of each part of the day   וּבְכָל שָׁעָה

with Your peace (which is a complete peace).   בִּשְׁלוֹמֶךָ.

ON SHABBOS SHUVAH THE FOLLOWING IS ADDED:

In the book of life (of ...)   בְּסֵפֶר חַיִּים

of abundant goodness and success   בְּרָכָה

and peace between a man and his friend   וְשָׁלוֹם

and a good (ample and easy) livelihood   וּפַרְנָסָה טוֹבָה

may we be remembered   נִזָּכֵר

and may we be inscribed before You   וְנִכָּתֵב לְפָנֶיךָ

we (who are standing together praying)   אֲנַחְנוּ

and all of Your nation, Israel   וְכָל עַמְּךָ בֵּית יִשְׂרָאֵל

(let us be remembered and inscribed) for a truly good life (i.e., a life that will enable us to earn the World to Come)   לְחַיִּים טוֹבִים

and for peace within ourselves (that we should be satisfied with the materialistic things that we have)   וּלְשָׁלוֹם

SOME SAY THE FOLLOWING CONCLUSION ON SHABBOS SHUVAH INSTEAD OF THE REGULAR CONCLUSION TO THE BLESSING

(You are the Source of Blessing, Master of all   (בָּרוּךְ אַתָּה יהוה

Who makes peace among all.)   עוֹשֶׂה הַשָּׁלוֹם.)

You are the Source of Blessing, Master of all   בָּרוּךְ אַתָּה יהוה

Who gives an abundance of goodness and   הַמְבָרֵךְ אֶת עַמּוֹ יִשְׂרָאֵל בַּשָּׁלוֹם.
success to His nation, Israel, with peace.

תחנונים
Personal Requests

The Master of all strength Who is able to do anything   אֱלֹהַי
and Who takes care of me with Divine Providence

help me to guard my tongue from speaking bad about   נְצוֹר לְשׁוֹנִי מֵרָע
others (*Lashon Hora*)

and [help me to guard] my lips from speaking   וּשְׂפָתַי מִדַּבֵּר מִרְמָה
deceit or falsehood

and help me so that my soul should be silent (that   וְלִמְקַלְלַי נַפְשִׁי תִדֹּם
even in thought I should not get angry) at those
who curse me

and help me so that my soul should be like dust   וְנַפְשִׁי כֶּעָפָר לַכֹּל תִּהְיֶה
(very humble) before everyone (and not mind
insults).

Open up my heart so that it should be receptive   פְּתַח לִבִּי בְּתוֹרָתֶךָ
and understand Your Torah

and help my soul eagerly pursue Your *mitzvos*   וּבְמִצְוֹתֶיךָ תִּרְדּוֹף נַפְשִׁי

and all those who want to harm me (whether in   וְכֹל הַחוֹשְׁבִים עָלַי רָעָה
mundane matters or spiritual matters, i.e., to
cause me to sin)

quickly annul their plan   מְהֵרָה הָפֵר עֲצָתָם

and ruin their thought (even before they make plans).	וְקַלְקֵל מַחֲשַׁבְתָּם
Act (take us out of exile) for the sake of Your Name, which is desecrated now among the gentiles	עֲשֵׂה לְמַעַן שְׁמֶךָ
act (take us out of exile) for the sake of Your right hand, which You have now withdrawn in our exile	עֲשֵׂה לְמַעַן יְמִינֶךָ
act (take us out of exile) for the sake of Your Holiness (so that all will know that You lead us with holiness)	עֲשֵׂה לְמַעַן קְדֻשָּׁתֶךָ
act (take us out of exile) for the sake of Your Torah (so the Torah can be studied properly and completely)	עֲשֵׂה לְמַעַן תּוֹרָתֶךָ
and in order that Your dear ones, Israel, should be released from all troubles	לְמַעַן יֵחָלְצוּן יְדִידֶיךָ
save them with (the wonders and miracles that are attributed to) Your right hand	הוֹשִׁיעָה יְמִינְךָ
and answer (even) me in this prayer.	וַעֲנֵנִי.
Let the words of my prayer be desirable to You[13]	יִהְיוּ לְרָצוֹן אִמְרֵי פִי
and also the thoughts of my heart which I cannot express [should be desirable] before You	וְהֶגְיוֹן לִבִּי לְפָנֶיךָ
Master of all	יהוה
My Rock, Whom I rely on for all my requests	צוּרִי
and Who will be my Redeemer.	וְגוֹאֲלִי.

---

13. *Seder Hayom* (quoted also in *Mishnah Berurah* 122:8) writes that one should say this verse with great concentration, for it will help a great deal that his prayers should not go unanswered.

One should bow and go back 3 steps like a servant departing from his master

The One Who makes peace in Heaven (among the angels)	**עֹשֶׂה שָׁלוֹם** בִּמְרוֹמָיו
may He make peace (for those on earth, who are naturally quarrelsome)	הוּא יַעֲשֶׂה שָׁלוֹם
on those of us here (praying together)	עָלֵינוּ
and on all of Israel	וְעַל כָּל יִשְׂרָאֵל
and (you, the angels who escort me,) agree to my prayer, and say Amen!	וְאִמְרוּ אָמֵן.
May it be Your desire	**יְהִי רָצוֹן** מִלְּפָנֶיךָ
Master of all	יהוה
the Master of all strength, Who is able to do anything and Who takes care of us with Divine Providence	אֱלֹהֵינוּ
and the God Who took care of our Fathers with Divine Providence	וֵאלֹהֵי אֲבוֹתֵינוּ
that You should rebuild the Temple (so that we will be able to do the ultimate *avodah* - service to You)	שֶׁיִּבָּנֶה בֵּית הַמִּקְדָּשׁ
quickly and in our lifetime	בִּמְהֵרָה בְיָמֵינוּ
and help us so that all our toil should be in learning Your Torah.	וְתֵן חֶלְקֵנוּ בְּתוֹרָתֶךָ.
And there, in the Temple, we will bring offerings (the ultimate service) with reverence	וְשָׁם נַעֲבָדְךָ בְּיִרְאָה
as [they brought offerings and served in reverence] in the earlier days (of Moshe)	כִּימֵי עוֹלָם
and as they did in the previous years (of Shlomo *Hamelech*).	וּכְשָׁנִים קַדְמוֹנִיּוֹת.
And then, it will be pleasing to the Master of all	וְעָרְבָה לַיהוה
the offerings that will be brought in the Temple (which is in the portion of Yehudah in Jerusalem)	מִנְחַת יְהוּדָה וִירוּשָׁלָיִם
as [the offerings were pleasing] in the earlier days (of Moshe)	כִּימֵי עוֹלָם
and as they were in the previous years (of Shlomo *Hamelech*).	וּכְשָׁנִים קַדְמוֹנִיּוֹת.

❧ ❧ ❧ ❧ ❧ ❧

מוסף לשבת
Musaf for Shabbos

When I call in the name of the Master of all   כִּי שֵׁם יהוה אֶקְרָא

you should ascribe greatness to the Master of all strength Who is able to do anything and Who takes care of us with Divine Providence   הָבוּ גֹדֶל לֵאלֹהֵינוּ :

Master of all — in particular, My Master   אֲדֹנָי

please open my lips (because I am afraid and ashamed to open them)   שְׂפָתַי תִּפְתָּח

and [help me pray with concentration, so] my mouth will [be able to] tell Your true praise   וּפִי יַגִּיד תְּהִלָּתֶךָ.

אבות
Our God and the God of Our Fathers, Who Created Everything, and Protected Abraham[1]

You are the source of blessing (an expression of praise)   **בָּרוּךְ** אַתָּה

Master of all (Who always was, is, and will be)   יהוה

the Master of all strength Who is able to do anything and Who takes care of us with Divine Providence   אֱלֹהֵינוּ

and the God Who took care of our Fathers with Divine Providence (and made a covenant with each of them)   וֵאלֹהֵי אֲבוֹתֵינוּ

the God Who made a covenant with our father Abraham (who excelled in kindness)   אֱלֹהֵי אַבְרָהָם

---

1 One must be very careful to concentrate when saying this *berachah*, because otherwise he does not fulfill his obligation to pray. In the time of the *Gemarah* one would have to repeat the *Shemoneh Esray* if he had not concentrated on it. Nowadays, however, when we are not sure that the second time will yield the proper concentration either, we do not repeat the *Shemoneh Esray*. However, the *Mishnah Berurah* [the authoritative *halachic* work] (101:4) states that if one did not yet say ברוך אתה ה' at the end of this *berachah*, he can go back to אלהי אברהם and repeat from there with concentration, thereby rectifying his previous lack of concentration.

the God Who made a covenant with our father Isaac (who excelled in service of God)	אֱלֹהֵי יִצְחָק
and the God Who made a covenant with our father Jacob (who excelled in learning Torah)	וֵאלֹהֵי יַעֲקֹב
He is the Almighty (all power is His, especially in exercising the attribute of mercy)	הָאֵל
Who is the Great One (all greatness is His, especially in exercising the attribute of kindness)	הַגָּדוֹל
(and) He is the Strong One (all strength is His, especially in exercising the attribute of judgment)	הַגִּבּוֹר
and He alone deserves to be feared (because no being has the ability to do good or bad except Him)	וְהַנּוֹרָא
for He is the supreme God Who is the ultimate cause of everything	אֵל עֶלְיוֹן
Who always does kindnesses that are purely good	גּוֹמֵל חֲסָדִים טוֹבִים
and He recreates everything, constantly, every day	וְקוֹנֶה הַכֹּל
and every day He recalls for our benefit the kindnesses performed by the forefathers	וְזוֹכֵר חַסְדֵי אָבוֹת
and He constantly brings the Redeemer closer	וּמֵבִיא גוֹאֵל
to the forefathers' childrens' children (even though the merit of the forefathers might already be used up)	לִבְנֵי בְנֵיהֶם
for the sake of His Name (which will be sanctified at the time of the Redemption)	לְמַעַן שְׁמוֹ
[and He will also bring the Redeemer] because of His great love for the Jewish people	בְּאַהֲבָה

Remember us for life in this world (in order that we may earn the World to Come by doing *mitzvos* here)	זָכְרֵנוּ לְחַיִּים
King, Who desires life (and not death for a sinner, but rather that he should repent)	מֶלֶךְ חָפֵץ בַּחַיִּים
and write us in the Book of the Righteous, for life	וְכָתְבֵנוּ בְּסֵפֶר הַחַיִּים
for Your sake, in order that we may serve You	לְמַעַנְךָ
the Master of all strength Who is able to do anything and is the One Who apportions life to all	אֱלֹהִים חַיִּים

He is the King over all   מֶלֶךְ

Who is the Helper (to help one succeed)   עוֹזֵר

and the Savior (from trouble)   וּמוֹשִׁיעַ

and the Protector (to prevent trouble from coming)   וּמָגֵן

You are the Source of Blessing, Master of all   בָּרוּךְ אַתָּה יהוה

the Protector of Abraham (and because of Abraham He continues His protection over us).   מָגֵן אַבְרָהָם:

גבורות

The Mighty Acts of God and the Revival of the Dead

You alone are eternally Strong   **אַתָּה** גִּבּוֹר לְעוֹלָם

Master of all   אֲדֹנָי

You even revive the dead (which shows the greatest strength, contradicting all laws of nature)   מְחַיֵּה מֵתִים אַתָּה

[and] You have an abundance of strength with which to save   רַב לְהוֹשִׁיעַ

He causes the wind to blow (which aids evaporation, blows clouds where they are needed, and facilitates all aspects of rain)	מַשִּׁיב הָרֽוּחַ
and He causes every drop of rain to fall on its desired place (and for its designated function: to nourish or to flood, etc.)	וּמוֹרִיד הַגֶּֽשֶׁם

He provides all the living with their food and other needs in kindness (not because they are deserving)	מְכַלְכֵּל חַיִּים בְּחֶֽסֶד
He revives the dead with great mercy (searching for merits with which they would deserve revival)	מְחַיֶּה מֵתִים בְּרַחֲמִים רַבִּים
He supports those who are falling (whether physically, emotionally, or financially)	סוֹמֵךְ נוֹפְלִים
and He heals the sick from all types of illnesses (even when doctors have given up hope)	וְרוֹפֵא חוֹלִים
and He opens the bonds of those who are restricted (e.g., giving movement to our limbs when we awaken)	וּמַתִּיר אֲסוּרִים
and He will keep His promise to those sleeping in the dust (the dead), to revive them.	וּמְקַיֵּם אֱמוּנָתוֹ לִישֵׁנֵי עָפָר
Who is like You (who can do as many mighty deeds, which are infinite, even for one person)?	מִי כָמֽוֹךָ
— You, to Whom all mighty deeds belong! —	בַּֽעַל גְּבוּרוֹת
And who is comparable to You in even one of Your mighty deeds (which are of the highest quality)?	וּמִי דֽוֹמֶה לָּךְ
You are the King over all	מֶֽלֶךְ
Who causes death and revival in many respects (such as sleep and awakening, poverty and wealth)	מֵמִית וּמְחַיֶּה
and, like the sprouting of a seed, You bring the Salvation (the Revival of the Dead)	וּמַצְמִיחַ יְשׁוּעָה

Who is like You, who has as much mercy on his sons as You, the Merciful Father, have for us

מִי כָמוֹךְ אַב הָרַחֲמִים

(and) remembers His creatures, out of mercy, for life

זוֹכֵר יְצוּרָיו לְחַיִּים בְּרַחֲמִים

And (from the mighty deeds that we mentioned) we see that You are surely trusted to revive the dead

וְנֶאֱמָן אַתָּה לְהַחֲיוֹת מֵתִים

You are the Source of Blessing, Master of all

בָּרוּךְ אַתָּה יהוה

the Reviver of all the dead (from Adam until the time of the Revival). [2]

מְחַיֵּה הַמֵּתִים:

קְדוּשַּׁת הַשֵּׁם
Holiness of God

You, Yourself, are holy (different and separate from everything)

אַתָּה קָדוֹשׁ

and Your Name (which comes from Your many acts) reveals holiness

וְשִׁמְךָ קָדוֹשׁ

and the holy ones — Israel

וּקְדוֹשִׁים

constantly praise You, every day, forever

בְּכָל יוֹם יְהַלְלוּךָ סֶּלָה

You are the Source of Blessing, Master of all

בָּרוּךְ אַתָּה יהוה

the Almighty, Who is holier than all else.

הָאֵל הַקָּדוֹשׁ.

the King Who is holier than all else.

הַמֶּלֶךְ הַקָּדוֹשׁ.

---

2. Even though many bodies have decomposed over thousands of years, and some have been burned and their dust has been scattered, and others have drowned at sea, *Hashem* with His great might will recognize and recompose the bodies and return to them their original souls (*Yesod Veshoresh Ha'avodah*).

קְדוּשַׁת הַיוֹם - קָרְבַּן מוּסָף
The Holiness of the Day and the *Korban Musaf*

ON A REGULAR SHABBOS SAY THE WORDS ABOVE THE LINE:

You established the Shabbos to rest on it   **תִּכַּנְתָּ** שַׁבָּת

(and) You wanted its sacrifices to be brought on it (although it would entail some otherwise forbidden activities)   רָצִיתָ קָרְבְּנוֹתֶיהָ

(and) You commanded (through Moshe) its explanations (i.e., exactly when the laws of Shabbos be set aside for sacrifices)   צִוִּיתָ פֵּרוּשֶׁיהָ

(and You commanded them) with their order of wine that was brought with it and poured on the altar for its *nesachim* (libations).   עִם סִדּוּרֵי נְסָכֶיהָ

Those who make the Shabbos a delight   מְעַנְּגֶיהָ

ON *SHABBOS ROSH CHODESH* THE FOLLOWING IS SAID INSTEAD:

You created Your world from the beginning (with great wisdom)   **אַתָּה יָצַרְתָּ** עוֹלָמְךָ מִקֶּדֶם

(and) You already completed Your work by the seventh day (Shabbos)   כִּלִּיתָ מְלַאכְתְּךָ בַּיּוֹם הַשְּׁבִיעִי

You showed Your love for us (by giving us the Torah)   אָהַבְתָּ אוֹתָנוּ

and You showed that You desired us (by giving us the special protection of the Clouds of Glory even though we had sinned with the golden calf)   וְרָצִיתָ בָּנוּ

and You elevated us from all languages (by giving us the holy language –Hebrew – which is spoken in Heaven)   וְרוֹמַמְתָּנוּ מִכָּל הַלְּשׁוֹנוֹת

and You made us holy by giving us the *mitzvos* which permeate us with holiness   וְקִדַּשְׁתָּנוּ בְּמִצְוֹתֶיךָ

and You have brought us close, our King, to Your service   וְקֵרַבְתָּנוּ מַלְכֵּנוּ לַעֲבוֹדָתֶךָ

will inherit honor forever (in the World to Come)   לְעוֹלָם כָּבוֹד יִנְחָלוּ

(and) those who honor it with different types of food and delicacies   טוֹעֲמֶיהָ

will merit long life   חַיִּים זָכוּ

and those who love its words (the laws of Shabbos)   וְגַם הָאוֹהֲבִים דְּבָרֶיהָ

have chosen great reward.[3]   גְּדֻלָּה בָּחָרוּ

At the beginning from Sinai we were commanded about Shabbos (in all its detail)   אָז מִסִּינַי נִצְטַוּוּ עָלֶיהָ

---

3. Those who keep and honor Shabbos will be on the highest level, as it is written (*Yeshayah* 58:14) concerning this: "and I [Hashem] will cause you to ride on the heights of the world" (*R' Shlomo ben Shimshon* from Worms [d. 1096]).

On Shabbos Rosh Chodesh

and Your Name which is great (as we see from Your acts)   וְשִׁמְךָ הַגָּדוֹל

and holy (as we see from Your running of the world with a mastery beyond our comprehension)   וְהַקָּדוֹשׁ

You have called on us—for we are called the Nation of God.   עָלֵינוּ קָרָאתָ:

And the Master of all, the Master of all strength Who is able to do anything and Who takes care of us with Divine Providence gave us   וַתִּתֶּן לָנוּ יהוה אֱלֹהֵינוּ

with love (because of His love for us)   בְּאַהֲבָה

Shabbosos to rest from all toil   שַׁבָּתוֹת לִמְנוּחָה

and *Rosh Chodesh* days for atonement (since on these days a sin offering was brought)   וְרָאשֵׁי חֳדָשִׁים לְכַפָּרָה

but because we and our forefathers have sinned before You   וּלְפִי שֶׁחָטָאנוּ לְפָנֶיךָ אֲנַחְנוּ וַאֲבוֹתֵינוּ

and You commanded us וְתִצַוֵּנוּ

Master of all, the Master of all strength Who is able to do יהוה אֱלֹהֵינוּ anything and Who takes care of us with Divine Providence

to sacrifice on Shabbos לְהַקְרִיב בָּהּ

the additional sacrifice for Shabbos, קָרְבַּן מוּסַף שַׁבָּת כָּרָאוּי according to its laws.

Let it be a favorable time before You to let יְהִי רָצוֹן מִלְּפָנֶיךָ our prayers enter the Heavens (to You)

Master of all, the Master of all strength Who is able to do יהוה אֱלֹהֵינוּ anything and Who takes care of us with Divine Providence

---

ON SHABBOS ROSH CHODESH

our city (Jerusalem) has been destroyed חָרְבָה עִירֵנוּ

and our Temple is desolate וְשָׁמֵם בֵּית מִקְדָּשֵׁנוּ

and our glory (the Divine Presence) has been exiled וְגָלָה יְקָרֵנוּ

and the honor (of sacrifices and prayers) has been taken וְנִטַּל כָּבוֹד

from the House of our life (the Temple) מִבֵּית חַיֵּינוּ

and we cannot bring the sacrifices וְאֵין אֲנַחְנוּ יְכוֹלִים לַעֲשׂוֹת חוֹבוֹתֵינוּ that we are obligated to

in the House where You chose to rest Your בְּבֵית בְּחִירָתֶךָ Divine Presence (the Temple)

which is the House that is great in a physical בַּבַּיִת הַגָּדוֹל וְהַקָּדוֹשׁ sense, and holy in a spiritual sense

on which Your name is called — for it is שֶׁנִּקְרָא שִׁמְךָ עָלָיו called the House of God —

because of the hand of the enemy that מִפְּנֵי הַיָּד שֶׁנִּשְׁתַּלְּחָה בְּמִקְדָּשֶׁךָ was sent to destroy Your Temple.

and the God Who took care of our Fathers
with Divine Providence

וֵאלֹהֵי אֲבוֹתֵינוּ

that You bring us up to our Land (Israel)
with joy

שֶׁתַּעֲלֵנוּ בְשִׂמְחָה לְאַרְצֵנוּ

and plant us (like a plant that cannot be uprooted)
within our borders (the borders of Israel)

וְתִטָּעֵנוּ בִּגְבוּלֵנוּ

and we will be able to bring before You
(in the Temple)

וְשָׁם נַעֲשֶׂה לְפָנֶיךָ

the sacrifices that are an obligation on
us (such as ...)

אֶת קָרְבְּנוֹת חוֹבוֹתֵינוּ

the daily *tamid* sacrifices in the order they are written
in the Torah (i.e. in the morning and afternoon)

תְּמִידִים כְּסִדְרָם

ON SHABBOS ROSH CHODESH

Let it be a favorable time before You to let our
prayers enter the Heavens (to You)

יְהִי רָצוֹן מִלְּפָנֶיךָ

Master of all, the Master of all strength Who is able to do
anything and Who takes care of us with Divine Providence

יהוה אֱלֹהֵינוּ

and the God who took care of our Fathers with
Divine Providence

וֵאלֹהֵי אֲבוֹתֵינוּ

that You bring us up to our Land (Israel) with joy

שֶׁתַּעֲלֵנוּ בְשִׂמְחָה לְאַרְצֵנוּ

and plant us (like a plant that cannot be uprooted)
within our borders (the borders of Israel)

וְתִטָּעֵנוּ בִּגְבוּלֵנוּ

and we will be able to bring before You (in the
Temple)

וְשָׁם נַעֲשֶׂה לְפָנֶיךָ

the sacrifices that are an obligation on us (such as ...)

אֶת קָרְבְּנוֹת חוֹבוֹתֵינוּ

the daily *tamid* sacrifices in the order they are written in
the Torah (i.e. in the morning and afternoon)

תְּמִידִים כְּסִדְרָם

and the additional *musaf* sacrifices according to their
laws that are written in the Torah

וּמוּסָפִים כְּהִלְכָתָם

and the *musaf* sacrifices of this Shabbos day

וְאֶת מוּסְפֵי יוֹם הַשַּׁבָּת הַזֶּה

and the additional *musaf* sacrifices according to their laws that are written in the Torah	וּמוּסָפִים כְּהִלְכָתָם
and the *musaf* sacrifices of this Shabbos day	וְאֶת מוּסַף יוֹם הַשַּׁבָּת הַזֶּה
we will do all the preparations of the sacrifices and bring them before You with love	נַעֲשֶׂה וְנַקְרִיב לְפָנֶיךָ בְּאַהֲבָה
as You commanded us	כְּמִצְוַת רְצוֹנֶךָ
as You wrote for us in Your Torah	כְּמוֹ שֶׁכָּתַבְתָּ עָלֵינוּ בְּתוֹרָתֶךָ
that Moshe wrote as a messenger of Yours	עַל יְדֵי משֶׁה עַבְדֶּךָ

<hr>

ON SHABBOS ROSH CHODESH

and the *musaf* sacrifices of this *Rosh Chodesh* day	וְיוֹם רֹאשׁ הַחֹדֶשׁ הַזֶּה
we will do all the preparations of the sacrifices and bring them before You with love	נַעֲשֶׂה וְנַקְרִיב לְפָנֶיךָ בְּאַהֲבָה
as You commanded us	כְּמִצְוַת רְצוֹנֶךָ
as You wrote for us in Your Torah	כְּמוֹ שֶׁכָּתַבְתָּ עָלֵינוּ בְּתוֹרָתֶךָ
that Moshe wrote as a messenger of Yours	עַל יְדֵי משֶׁה עַבְדֶּךָ
just as he heard from the mouth of Your Honor	מִפִּי כְבוֹדֶךָ
as it is written (*Bamidbar* 28:9-11):	כָּאָמוּר:
And (the *korban musaf* of) the day of Shabbos is	**וּבְיוֹם** הַשַּׁבָּת
two sheep within their first year, that do not have any blemishes	שְׁנֵי כְבָשִׂים בְּנֵי שָׁנָה תְּמִימִם

just as he heard from the mouth of Your Honor

מִפִּי כְבוֹדֶךָ

as it is written (*Bamidbar* 28:9-10):

כָּאָמוּר:

And (the *korban musaf* of) the day of Shabbos is

וּבְיוֹם הַשַּׁבָּת

two sheep within their first year, that do not have any blemishes

שְׁנֵי כְבָשִׂים בְּנֵי שָׁנָה תְּמִימִם

and two-tenths of an *eifah* (a measure) of the finest wheat flour for a *korban minchah*

וּשְׁנֵי עֶשְׂרוֹנִים סֹלֶת מִנְחָה

mixed with olive-oil

בְּלוּלָה בַשֶּׁמֶן

ON SHABBOS ROSH CHODESH

and two-tenths of an *eifah* (a measure) of the finest wheat flour for a *korban minchah*

וּשְׁנֵי עֶשְׂרוֹנִים סֹלֶת מִנְחָה

mixed with olive-oil

בְּלוּלָה בַשֶּׁמֶן

and wine to pour on the altar for its *nesachim* (libations).

וְנִסְכּוֹ.

This was the *olah* of the *korbon musaf* for every Shabbos

עֹלַת שַׁבַּת בְּשַׁבַּתּוֹ

which was sacrificed after the *olah* of the *korbon tamid*

עַל עֹלַת הַתָּמִיד

and the wine that was brought with it and poured on the altar for its *nesachim*.

וְנִסְכָּהּ.

SOME SAY:
(This is the *korban musaf* of Shabbos, and the *korban musaf* of Rosh Chodesh is as it is written in the Torah:)

SOME SAY:
(זֶה קָרְבַּן שַׁבָּת וְקָרְבַּן הַיּוֹם כָּאָמוּר:)

And on your *Rosh Chodesh* days

וּבְרָאשֵׁי חָדְשֵׁיכֶם

you should bring a *Korban Olah* to be consumed on the Altar for the Master of all

תַּקְרִיבוּ עֹלָה לַיהוה

and wine to pour on the altar for its *nesachim*.	וְנִסְכּוֹ.
This was the *olah* of the *korbon musaf* for every Shabbos	עֹלַת שַׁבַּת בְּשַׁבַּתּוֹ
which was sacrificed after the *olah* of the *korbon tamid*	עַל עֹלַת הַתָּמִיד
and the wine that was brought with it and poured on the altar for its *nesachim*.	וְנִסְכָּהּ.
They will rejoice in the revelation of Your Kingdom (in the future)	**יִשְׂמְחוּ** בְמַלְכוּתֶךָ
those who keep Shabbos (by ceasing from their work on Shabbos)	שׁוֹמְרֵי שַׁבָּת

ON SHABBOS ROSH CHODESH

two young bulls (from the beginning of their second year until the end of their third year)	פָּרִים בְּנֵי בָקָר שְׁנַיִם
and one ram (more than thirteen months old)	וְאַיִל אֶחָד
(and) seven male sheep in their first year	כְּבָשִׂים בְּנֵי שָׁנָה שִׁבְעָה
(all of which had to be) without blemish.	תְּמִימִם :
And their accompanying flour offerings and wine libations are as mentioned in the Torah	וּמִנְחָתָם וְנִסְכֵּיהֶם כִּמְדֻבָּר
three-tenths of an *eifah* of fine flour for the bull	שְׁלֹשָׁה עֶשְׂרֹנִים לַפָּר
and two-tenths of an *eifah* of fine flour for the ram	וּשְׁנֵי עֶשְׂרֹנִים לָאָיִל
and one-tenth of an *eifah* of fine flour for each of the seven sheep	וְעִשָּׂרוֹן לַכֶּבֶשׂ
and wine for each one according to the amount prescribed in the Torah to pour on the altar;	וְיַיִן כְּנִסְכּוֹ
and a male goat within its first year as the sin offering of the *musaf* to atone for *tumah*[4] in the Temple	וְשָׂעִיר לְכַפֵּר

---

4. This refers to spiritual impurity, and like all *musaf* goats, these come to atone for a spiritually impure person who either entered the Temple or ate from an offering (*Rashi, Bamidbar* 28:15).

and call it a delight (by having food, drink and delicacies for Shabbos).   וְקוֹרְאֵי עֹנֶג

The nation (Israel) who makes the seventh day (Shabbos) holy (by not working on it)   עַם מְקַדְּשֵׁי שְׁבִיעִי

they will all be satisfied and still delight from Your spiritual good (in the future)   כֻּלָּם יִשְׂבְּעוּ וְיִתְעַנְּגוּ מִטּוּבֶךְ

for in the seventh day You were pleased and made it holy (to be a day of rest from work)   וּבַשְּׁבִיעִי רָצִיתָ בּוֹ וְקִדַּשְׁתּוֹ

(and) to be the most desirable day of the week   חֶמְדַּת יָמִים

(and) You called it "Shabbos"   אוֹתוֹ קָרָאתָ

ON SHABBOS ROSH CHODESH

and the two daily sacrifices (one in the morning and one in the afternoon)   וּשְׁנֵי תְמִידִים

according to their laws that are written in the Torah.   כְּהִלְכָתָם.

They will rejoice in the revelation of Your Kingdom (in the future)   **יִשְׂמְחוּ** בְמַלְכוּתְךָ

those who keep Shabbos (by ceasing from their work on Shabbos)   שׁוֹמְרֵי שַׁבָּת

and call it a delight (by having food, drink and delicacies for Shabbos).   וְקוֹרְאֵי עֹנֶג

The nation (Israel) who makes the seventh day (Shabbos) holy (by not working on it)   עַם מְקַדְּשֵׁי שְׁבִיעִי

they will all be satisfied and still delight from Your spiritual good (in the future)   כֻּלָּם יִשְׂבְּעוּ וְיִתְעַנְּגוּ מִטּוּבֶךְ

for in the seventh day You were pleased and made it holy (to be a day of rest from work)   וּבַשְּׁבִיעִי רָצִיתָ בּוֹ וְקִדַּשְׁתּוֹ

(and) to be the most desirable day of the week   חֶמְדַּת יָמִיח

as a remembrance to the work of creation
(that He ceased from work on the seventh day).

זֵכֶר לְמַעֲשֵׂה בְרֵאשִׁית.

The Master of all strength Who is able to do anything
and Who takes care of us with Divine Providence

אֱלֹהֵינוּ

and the God Who took care of our Fathers with
Divine Providence

וֵאלֹהֵי אֲבוֹתֵינוּ

let our rest be pleasant before You

רְצֵה בִמְנוּחָתֵנוּ

make us holy from Above so that we should keep
Your mitzvos properly

קַדְּשֵׁנוּ בְּמִצְוֹתֶיךָ

and grant us Divine assistance that all of our
occupation should be in Torah study

וְתֵן חֶלְקֵנוּ בְּתוֹרָתֶךָ

ON SHABBOS ROSH CHODESH

(and) You called it "Shabbos"

אוֹתוֹ קָרָאתָ

as a remembrance to the work of creation (that He
ceased from work on the seventh day).

זֵכֶר לְמַעֲשֵׂה בְרֵאשִׁית.

The Master of all strength Who is able to do anything and
Who takes care of us with Divine Providence

אֱלֹהֵינוּ

and the God Who took care of our Fathers with
Divine Providence

וֵאלֹהֵי אֲבוֹתֵינוּ

let our rest be pleasant before You

רְצֵה בִמְנוּחָתֵנוּ

and renew on our behalf on this Shabbos day

וְחַדֵּשׁ עָלֵינוּ בְּיוֹם הַשַּׁבָּת הַזֶּה

this (new) month

אֶת הַחֹדֶשׁ הַזֶּה

(and grant what is) good for each person as well as
prosperity and success

לְטוֹבָה וְלִבְרָכָה

(and that we should have) extraordinary joy as well
as joy from common things

לְשָׂשׂוֹן וּלְשִׂמְחָה

bestow upon us good in a way that we will be satisfied with what we have (and not pursue our desires)   שַׂבְּעֵנוּ מִטּוּבֶךְ

and cause us to rejoice through the salvation that You will bring us   וְשַׂמְּחֵנוּ בִּישׁוּעָתֶךְ

and (we ask that You) purify our hearts so that we serve You sincerely (without other motives)   וְטַהֵר לִבֵּנוּ לְעָבְדְּךָ בֶּאֱמֶת

and give us as an inheritance (the holiness that Shabbos inspires)   וְהַנְחִילֵנוּ

Master of all, the Master of all strength Who is able to do anything and Who takes care of us with Divine Providence   יהוה אֱלֹהֵינוּ

because of the love that You have for us (by giving us Shabbos)   בְּאַהֲבָה

ON SHABBOS ROSH CHODESH

(and that it should be a time) for salvation from our exile as well as comfort from our troubles   לִישׁוּעָה וּלְנֶחָמָה

(that we should have in it) all our needs (such as clothing) and food   לְפַרְנָסָה וּלְכַלְכָּלָה

(that we should have in it) life and peace   לְחַיִּים וּלְשָׁלוֹם

(that we should have in it) forgiveness of the punishment for our unintentional sins   לִמְחִילַת חֵטְא

as well as forgiveness for the actual sin for intentional sins   וְלִסְלִיחַת עָוֹן

IN A JEWISH LEAP YEAR THROUGH ADAR SHENI ADD THE FOLLOWING LINE:

(and to atone completely [entirely wipe out any trace] from our rebellious sins.)   (וּלְכַפָּרַת פֶּשַׁע)

(Do all these) because You have chosen Israel to be Your nation from among all the nations   כִּי בְעַמְּךָ יִשְׂרָאֵל בָּחַרְתָּ מִכָּל הָאֻמּוֹת

and the special qualities of Shabbos, Your holy day, You made known only to them   וְשַׁבַּת קָדְשְׁךָ לָהֶם הוֹדָעְתָּ

and because of the desire You have for us (that
You want us to bring sacrifices even on Shabbos)

וּבִרְצוֹן

[give us as an inheritance] (the inspiration of)
Shabbos that You made holy

שַׁבַּת קָדְשֶׁךָ

and (through this inspiration) You should cause
Israel to have a complete rest on Shabbos

וְיָנוּחוּ בוֹ יִשְׂרָאֵל

for they sanctify Your Name (by keeping
Shabbos)

מְקַדְּשֵׁי שְׁמֶךָ

You are the Source of Blessing, Master of all

בָּרוּךְ אַתָּה יהוה

Who made the Shabbos holier (than the other
days — and gave it to us as a present).[5]

מְקַדֵּשׁ הַשַּׁבָּת.

---

5. One should concentrate at this point on giving great praise and thanks to Hashem for
   this great gift of Shabbos, and he should give this thanks with great joy. (*Yesod
   Veshoresh Ha'avodah*)

ON SHABBOS ROSH CHODESH

and You established for them the laws of the
new moons (that Israel should count according
to them)

וְחֻקֵּי רָאשֵׁי חֳדָשִׁים לָהֶם קָבָעְתָּ

You are the Source of Blessing, Master of all

בָּרוּךְ אַתָּה יהוה

Who made the Shabbos holier (than the other days — and
gave it to us as a present)

מְקַדֵּשׁ הַשַּׁבָּת

and made Israel holier (than the other nations)

וְיִשְׂרָאֵל

and (through Israel He makes holy) the New Moons[6].

וְרָאשֵׁי חֳדָשִׁים:

---

6. One should concentrate at this point on giving great praise and thanks to Hashem for all these
   three benefits: that He gave us the hidden gift of Shabbos, that He chose us from all the nations,
   and that He gave us the great present of *Rosh Chodesh*. (*Yesod Veshoresh Ha'avodah*)

עבודה
Return of the Temple Service

Be pleased[7]	רְצֵה
Master of all	יהוה
the Master of all strength, Who is able to do anything and Who takes care of us with Divine Providence	אֱלֹהֵינוּ
with Your nation, Israel (because they are praying for the rebuilding of the Temple)	בְּעַמְּךָ יִשְׂרָאֵל
and with their prayer (for the rebuilding of the Temple)	וּבִתְפִלָּתָם
and return the service of the Temple	וְהָשֵׁב אֶת הָעֲבוֹדָה
(even) to the Holy of Holies.	לִדְבִיר בֵּיתֶךָ
And the fire-offerings that they will bring	וְאִשֵּׁי יִשְׂרָאֵל
and the prayer of Israel (which is now in place of the offerings)	וּתְפִלָּתָם
because of Your love for the Jews	בְּאַהֲבָה
accept with desire	תְקַבֵּל בְּרָצוֹן

---

7. Before this blessing one should instill in his heart love of all Jews, no matter what country or group they belong to, for we ask God here that He should be pleased with all of His nation, Israel (*Darchay Chayim*). [The saintly Chofetz Chaim wrote in *Ahavas Yisrael* (Ch. 2) that we pray constantly for the rebuilding of the Temple, but we don't contemplate the cause of its destruction, which was hatred for an unjustifiable reason. Therefore if we want the Temple to be rebuilt we first must rectify this sin and love all Jews.]

and help us that it should always be desirable	וּתְהִי לְרָצוֹן תָּמִיד
the service (whether offerings or prayers) of Israel, Your nation	עֲבוֹדַת יִשְׂרָאֵל עַמֶּךָ
and let us merit to see (the *Shechinah* — Divine Presence) with our own eyes (i.e., soon, in our days)	**וְתֶחֱזֶינָה** עֵינֵינוּ
when You return Your Presence to the Temple (even if it is) in mercy (and not through our merits)	בְּשׁוּבְךָ לְצִיּוֹן בְּרַחֲמִים
You are the Source of Blessing, Master of all	בָּרוּךְ אַתָּה יהוה
Who will return His Divine Presence to the Temple.	הַמַּחֲזִיר שְׁכִינָתוֹ לְצִיּוֹן.

הודאה
Thanking God[8]

We give thanks to You, acknowledging	**מוֹדִים** אֲנַחְנוּ לָךְ
that You are the Master of all	שָׁאַתָּה הוּא יהוה
the Master of all strength, Who is able to do anything and Who takes care of us with Divine Providence	אֱלֹהֵינוּ
and the God Who took care of our Fathers with Divine Providence	וֵאלֹהֵי אֲבוֹתֵינוּ
(and that You will continue to take care of us) forever	לְעוֹלָם וָעֶד
[You are] the Rock — Creator and Sustainer — of our lives	צוּר חַיֵּינוּ

---

8. The *Bais Elokim* explains that the reason we bow at the beginning and end of this *berachah* is to show humility, recognizing our unworthiness for *Hashem's* special care, and realizing that all our lives and all goodness come from Him.

[and You are] the Protector Who saves us from all troubles   מָגֵן יִשְׁעֵנוּ

You are the One [Who keeps us alive and saves us] in every generation.   אַתָּה הוּא לְדוֹר וָדוֹר

We will always express our thanks to You   נוֹדֶה לְּךָ

and we will tell Your praise to others   וּנְסַפֵּר תְּהִלָּתֶךָ

for our lives — each breath — that is given over into Your hand   עַל חַיֵּינוּ הַמְּסוּרִים בְּיָדֶךָ

and for our souls that are entrusted to You (while we sleep)   וְעַל נִשְׁמוֹתֵינוּ הַפְּקוּדוֹת לָךְ

and for the hidden miracles that You do for us every day   וְעַל נִסֶּיךָ שֶׁבְּכָל יוֹם עִמָּנוּ

and for Your wonders of "nature" (which You renew constantly)   וְעַל נִפְלְאוֹתֶיךָ

and for Your favors (that You do for us constantly)   וְטוֹבוֹתֶיךָ

that You do in all parts of the day   שֶׁבְּכָל עֵת

in the evening, morning, and afternoon.   עֶרֶב וָבֹקֶר וְצָהֳרָיִם

You are the ultimate Good One   הַטּוֹב

for Your mercy has never finished — for You withhold punishment from those deserving it   כִּי לֹא כָלוּ רַחֲמֶיךָ

and You are the ultimate Merciful One (Who not only withholds punishment, but....)   וְהַמְרַחֵם

Whose kindness never ends — for You even give these undeserving people additional kindnesses   כִּי לֹא תַמּוּ חֲסָדֶיךָ

we have always put our hope in You.

מֵעוֹלָם קִוִּינוּ לָךְ

ON CHANUKAH AND PURIM ONE ADDS על הנסים FOUND ON P. 90.

And for all of these wonders and favors that You do
for us constantly

וְעַל כֻּלָּם

[Your Name] should be praised with the recognition
that You are the Source of all Blessing

יִתְבָּרַךְ

and may Your Name (which represents Your acts) be
exalted through the recognition of Your greatness

וְיִתְרוֹמַם שִׁמְךָ

since You are our King (Who takes care of us especially)
[we desire that Your Name be praised and exalted]

מַלְכֵּנוּ

constantly, every day

תָּמִיד

forever and ever.

לְעוֹלָם וָעֶד.

ON SHABBOS SHUVAH THE FOLLOWING IS ADDED:

And inscribe for a good life (i.e., life that will
be good for earning the World to Come)

וּכְתוֹב לְחַיִּים טוֹבִים

all the children of Your covenant

כָּל בְּנֵי בְרִיתֶךָ

And all the living (those who will come back
to life by the Revival of the Dead)

וְכֹל הַחַיִּים

will thank You constantly forever

יוֹדוּךָ סֶּלָה

and they will praise Your Name (which
comes from Your deeds) truthfully, without
any other motive

וִיהַלְלוּ אֶת שִׁמְךָ בֶּאֱמֶת

the Almighty

הָאֵל

Who saves us in all our troubles

יְשׁוּעָתֵנוּ

and Who helps us to succeed

וְעֶזְרָתֵנוּ

constantly, forever

סֶלָה

You are the Source of Blessing, Master of all

בָּרוּךְ אַתָּה יהוה

Whose Name is "The Good One" (for You
are the ultimate good)

הַטּוֹב שִׁמְךָ

and to You alone is it fitting to give thanks
(because You are the cause of all goodness).

וּלְךָ נָאֶה לְהוֹדוֹת.

שלום
Peace[9]

Grant peace (which includes peace of mind, peace in
one's house, peace between Jews, and peace in one's
country)

שִׂים שָׁלוֹם

(and grant what is) good for each person

טוֹבָה

and (grant) prosperity and success

וּבְרָכָה

(and) let us find favor in Your eyes and thereby find favor
in the eyes of all who see us

חֵן

and grant our requests (even though we are not
deserving)

וָחֶסֶד

and have mercy on us (not to punish us according
to our wrongdoings)

וְרַחֲמִים

---

9. The last *mishnah* states that God found no adequate vehicle for Israel's blessing
other than peace. The Sages tell us (*Vayikra Rabbah* 9:9) that peace is so great that
it comes at the end of all prayers. As the *Seder Hayom* [R' Moshe ben Yehuda
Machir (16th cent.)] writes, "Peace encompasses everything and through peace we
will merit everything." Therefore, one should concentrate especially on this all-
encompassing final *berachah*.

on those of us here (praying together)

עָלֵינוּ

and on all of Israel, Your nation.

וְעַל כָּל יִשְׂרָאֵל עַמֶּךָ

Since You are our Father, give us an abundance of goodness and success

בָּרְכֵנוּ אָבִינוּ

all of us like one (equally)

כֻּלָּנוּ כְּאֶחָד

with the "light of Your face" (which is a symbol of Your great love)

בְּאוֹר פָּנֶיךָ

because, as we already know from the Revelation at Sinai, that with the "light of Your face" come great things:

כִּי בְאוֹר פָּנֶיךָ

You gave to us as a present (not because we were deserving),

נָתַתָּ לָּנוּ

Master of all

יהוה

the Master of all strength, Who is able to do anything and Who takes care of us with Divine Providence,

אֱלֹהֵינוּ

the Torah that teaches us how to live

תּוֹרַת חַיִּים

and (through it) the love of doing kindness

וְאַהֲבַת חֶסֶד

and (You gave us with the Torah more opportunities for) reward in the World to Come (by fulfilling the many *mitzvos*)

וּצְדָקָה

and (as reward for keeping the Torah You give us also) an abundance of goodness and success (in this world)

וּבְרָכָה

and (in the merit of keeping the Torah You give us) special mercy

וְרַחֲמִים

and (as a reward for keeping the Torah You give us) a long, healthy life

וְחַיִּים

and (through the Torah we have) peace of body and mind (because all the ways of the Torah are peaceful)	וְשָׁלוֹם
And it should be good in Your eyes	וְטוֹב בְּעֵינֶיךָ
to give an abundance of goodness and success to Your nation, Israel	לְבָרֵךְ אֶת עַמְּךָ יִשְׂרָאֵל
in all parts of the day	בְּכָל עֵת
and in all hours of each part of the day	וּבְכָל שָׁעָה
with Your peace (which is a complete peace).	בִּשְׁלוֹמֶךָ.

ON SHABBOS SHUVA THE FOLLOWING IS ADDED:

In the book of life (of …)	בְּסֵפֶר חַיִּים
of abundant goodness and success	בְּרָכָה
and peace between a man and his friend	וְשָׁלוֹם
and a good (ample and easy) livelihood	וּפַרְנָסָה טוֹבָה
may we be remembered	נִזָּכֵר
and may we be inscribed before You	וְנִכָּתֵב לְפָנֶיךָ
we (who are standing together praying)	אֲנַחְנוּ
and all of Your nation, Israel	וְכָל עַמְּךָ בֵּית יִשְׂרָאֵל
(let us be remembered and inscribed) for a truly good life (i.e., a life that will enable us to earn the World to Come)	לְחַיִּים טוֹבִים
and for peace within ourselves (that we should be satisfied with the materialistic things that we have)	וּלְשָׁלוֹם

SOME SAY THE FOLLOWING CONCLUSION ON SHABBOS SHUVAH
INSTEAD OF THE REGULAR CONCLUSION TO THE BLESSING

(You are the Source of Blessing, Master of all	(בָּרוּךְ אַתָּה יהוה
Who makes peace among all.)	עוֹשֶׂה הַשָּׁלוֹם.)

You are the Source of Blessing, Master of all	בָּרוּךְ אַתָּה יהוה
Who gives an abundance of goodness and success to His nation, Israel, with peace.	הַמְבָרֵךְ אֶת עַמּוֹ יִשְׂרָאֵל בַּשָּׁלוֹם.

תחנונים
Personal Requests

The Master of all strength Who is able to do anything and Who takes care of me with Divine Providence	אֱלֹהַי
help me to guard my tongue from speaking bad about others (*Lashon Hora*)	נְצוֹר לְשׁוֹנִי מֵרָע
and [help me to guard] my lips from speaking deceit or falsehood	וּשְׂפָתַי מִדַּבֵּר מִרְמָה
and help me so that my soul should be silent (that even in thought I should not get angry) at those who curse me	וְלִמְקַלְלַי נַפְשִׁי תִדֹּם
and help me so that my soul should be like dust (very humble) before everyone (and not mind insults).	וְנַפְשִׁי כֶּעָפָר לַכֹּל תִּהְיֶה
Open up my heart so that it should be receptive and understand Your Torah	פְּתַח לִבִּי בְּתוֹרָתֶךָ
and help my soul eagerly pursue Your *mitzvos*	וּבְמִצְוֹתֶיךָ תִּרְדּוֹף נַפְשִׁי
and all those who want to harm me (whether in mundane matters or spiritual matters, i.e., to cause me to sin)	וְכֹל הַחוֹשְׁבִים עָלַי רָעָה
quickly annul their plan	מְהֵרָה הָפֵר עֲצָתָם
and ruin their thought (even before they make plans).	וְקַלְקֵל מַחֲשַׁבְתָּם

Act (take us out of exile) for the sake of Your Name, which is desecrated now among the gentiles   עֲשֵׂה לְמַעַן שְׁמֶךָ

act (take us out of exile) for the sake of Your right hand, which You have now withdrawn in our exile   עֲשֵׂה לְמַעַן יְמִינֶךָ

act (take us out of exile) for the sake of Your Holiness (so that all will know that You lead us with holiness)   עֲשֵׂה לְמַעַן קְדֻשָּׁתֶךָ

act (take us out of exile) for the sake of Your Torah (so the Torah can be studied properly and completely)   עֲשֵׂה לְמַעַן תּוֹרָתֶךָ

and in order that Your dear ones, Israel, should be released from all troubles   לְמַעַן יֵחָלְצוּן יְדִידֶיךָ

save them with (the wonders and miracles that are attributed to) Your right hand   הוֹשִׁיעָה יְמִינְךָ

and answer (even) me in this prayer.   וַעֲנֵנִי.

Let the words of my prayer be desirable to You[10]   יִהְיוּ לְרָצוֹן אִמְרֵי פִי

and also the thoughts of my heart which I cannot express [should be desirable] before You   וְהֶגְיוֹן לִבִּי לְפָנֶיךָ

Master of all   יהוה

My Rock, Whom I rely on for all my requests   צוּרִי

and Who will be my Redeemer.   וְגוֹאֲלִי.

ONE SHOULD BOW AND GO BACK 3 STEPS LIKE A SERVANT DEPARTING FROM HIS MASTER

---

10. *Seder Hayom* (quoted also in *Mishnah Berurah* 122:8) writes that one should say this verse with great concentration, for it will help a great deal that his prayers should not go unanswered.

The One Who makes peace in Heaven (among the angels)	**עֹשֶׂה שָׁלוֹם** בִּמְרוֹמָיו
may He make peace (for those on earth, who are naturally quarrelsome)	הוּא יַעֲשֶׂה שָׁלוֹם
on those of us here (praying together)	עָלֵינוּ
and on all of Israel	וְעַל כָּל יִשְׂרָאֵל
and (you, the angels who escort me,) agree to my prayer, and say Amen!	וְאִמְרוּ אָמֵן.
May it be Your desire	**יְהִי רָצוֹן** מִלְּפָנֶיךָ
Master of all	יהוה
the Master of all strength, Who is able to do anything and Who takes care of us with Divine Providence	אֱלֹהֵינוּ
and the God Who took care of our Fathers with Divine Providence	וֵאלֹהֵי אֲבוֹתֵינוּ
that You should rebuild the Temple (so that we will be able to do the ultimate *avodah* - service to You)	שֶׁיִּבָּנֶה בֵּית הַמִּקְדָּשׁ
quickly and in our lifetime	בִּמְהֵרָה בְיָמֵינוּ
and help us so that all our toil should be in learning Your Torah.	וְתֵן חֶלְקֵנוּ בְּתוֹרָתֶךָ.
And there, in the Temple, we will bring offerings (the ultimate service) with reverence	וְשָׁם נַעֲבָדְךָ בְּיִרְאָה
as [they brought offerings and served in reverence] in the earlier days (of Moshe)	כִּימֵי עוֹלָם
and as they did in the previous years (of Shlomo *Hamelech*).	וּכְשָׁנִים קַדְמוֹנִיּוֹת.
And then, it will be pleasing to the Master of all	וְעָרְבָה לַיהוה
the offerings that will be brought in the Temple (which is in the portion of Yehudah in Jerusalem)	מִנְחַת יְהוּדָה וִירוּשָׁלָיִם
as [the offerings were pleasing] in the earlier days (of Moshe)	כִּימֵי עוֹלָם
and as they were in the previous years (of Shlomo *Hamelech*).	וּכְשָׁנִים קַדְמוֹנִיּוֹת.

מנחה לשבת
Minchah for Shabbos

When I call in the name of the Master of all	**כִּי** שֵׁם יהוה אֶקְרָא
you should ascribe greatness to the Master of all strength Who is able to do anything and Who takes care of us with Divine Providence	הָבוּ גֹדֶל לֵאלֹהֵינוּ :
Master of all — in particular, My Master	אֲדֹנָי
please open my lips (because I am afraid and ashamed to open them)	שְׂפָתַי תִּפְתָּח
and [help me pray with concentration, so] my mouth will [be able to] tell Your true praise	וּפִי יַגִּיד תְּהִלָּתֶךָ.

אבות
Our God and the God of Our Fathers, Who Created Everything, and Protected Abraham[1]

You are the source of blessing (an expression of praise)	**בָּרוּךְ** אַתָּה
Master of all (Who always was, is, and will be)	יהוה
the Master of all strength Who is able to do anything and Who takes care of us with Divine Providence	אֱלֹהֵינוּ
and the God Who took care of our Fathers with Divine Providence (and made a covenant with each of them)	וֵאלֹהֵי אֲבוֹתֵינוּ
the God Who made a covenant with our father Abraham (who excelled in kindness)	אֱלֹהֵי אַבְרָהָם

---

1. One must be very careful to concentrate when saying this *berachah*, because otherwise he does not fulfill his obligation to pray. In the time of the *Gemarah* one would have to repeat the *Shemoneh Esray* if he had not concentrated on it. Nowadays, however, when we are not sure that the second time will yield the proper concentration either, we do not repeat the *Shemoneh Esray*. However, the *Mishnah Berurah* [the authoritative *halachic* work] (101.4) states that if one did not yet say ברוך אתה ה׳ at the end of this *berachah*, he can go back to אלהי אברהם and repeat from there with concentration, thereby rectifying his previous lack of concentration.

the God Who made a covenant with our father Isaac (who excelled in service of God)	אֱלֹהֵי יִצְחָק
and the God Who made a covenant with our father Jacob (who excelled in learning Torah)	וֵאלֹהֵי יַעֲקֹב
He is the Almighty (all power is His, especially in exercising the attribute of mercy)	הָאֵל
Who is the Great One (all greatness is His, especially in exercising the attribute of kindness)	הַגָּדוֹל
(and) He is the Strong One (all strength is His, especially in exercising the attribute of judgment)	הַגִּבּוֹר
and He alone deserves to be feared (because no being has the ability to do good or bad except Him)	וְהַנּוֹרָא
for He is the supreme God Who is the ultimate cause of everything	אֵל עֶלְיוֹן
Who always does kindnesses that are purely good	גּוֹמֵל חֲסָדִים טוֹבִים
and He recreates everything, constantly, every day	וְקוֹנֵה הַכֹּל
and every day He recalls for our benefit the kindnesses performed by the forefathers	וְזוֹכֵר חַסְדֵי אָבוֹת
and He constantly brings the Redeemer closer	וּמֵבִיא גוֹאֵל
to the forefathers' childrens' children (even though the merit of the forefathers might already be used up)	לִבְנֵי בְנֵיהֶם
for the sake of His Name (which will be sanctified at the time of the Redemption)	לְמַעַן שְׁמוֹ
[and He will also bring the Redeemer] because of His great love for the Jewish people	בְּאַהֲבָה

Remember us for life in this world (in order that we may earn the World to Come by doing *mitzvos* here)	זָכְרֵנוּ לְחַיִּים
King, Who desires life (and not death for a sinner, but rather that he should repent)	מֶלֶךְ חָפֵץ בַּחַיִּים
and write us in the Book of the Righteous, for life	וְכָתְבֵנוּ בְּסֵפֶר הַחַיִּים
for Your sake, in order that we may serve You	לְמַעַנְךָ
the Master of all strength Who is able to do anything and is the One Who apportions life to all	אֱלֹהִים חַיִּים

He is the King over all   מֶלֶךְ

Who is the Helper (to help one succeed)   עוֹזֵר

and the Savior (from trouble)   וּמוֹשִׁיעַ

and the Protector (to prevent trouble from coming)   וּמָגֵן

You are the Source of Blessing, Master of all   בָּרוּךְ אַתָּה יהוה

the Protector of Abraham (and because of Abraham He continues His protection over us).   מָגֵן אַבְרָהָם:

גבורות

The Mighty Acts of God and the Revival of the Dead

You alone are eternally Strong   **אַתָּה** גִּבּוֹר לְעוֹלָם

Master of all   אֲדֹנָי

You even revive the dead (which shows the greatest strength, contradicting all laws of nature)   מְחַיֵּה מֵתִים אַתָּה

[and] You have an abundance of strength with which to save   רַב לְהוֹשִׁיעַ

FROM *MUSAF* OF *SHEMINI ATSERES* UNTIL AFTER *MUSAF* OF THE FIRST DAY OF *PESACH*, SAY:

He causes the wind to blow (which aids evaporation, blows clouds where they are needed, and facilitates all aspects of rain)	מַשִּׁיב הָרוּחַ
and He causes every drop of rain to fall on its desired place (and for its designated function: to nourish or to flood, etc.)	וּמוֹרִיד הַגֶּשֶׁם

He provides all the living with their food and other needs in kindness (not because they are deserving)

מְכַלְכֵּל חַיִּים בְּחֶסֶד

He revives the dead with great mercy (searching for merits with which they would deserve revival)

מְחַיֶּה מֵתִים בְּרַחֲמִים רַבִּים

He supports those who are falling (whether physically, emotionally, or financially)

סוֹמֵךְ נוֹפְלִים

and He heals the sick from all types of illnesses (even when doctors have given up hope)

וְרוֹפֵא חוֹלִים

and He opens the bonds of those who are restricted (e.g., giving movement to our limbs when we awaken)

וּמַתִּיר אֲסוּרִים

and He will keep His promise to those sleeping in the dust (the dead), to revive them.

וּמְקַיֵּם אֱמוּנָתוֹ לִישֵׁנֵי עָפָר

Who is like You (who can do as many mighty deeds, which are infinite, even for one person)?

מִי כָמוֹךָ

— You, to Whom all mighty deeds belong! —

בַּעַל גְּבוּרוֹת

And who is comparable to You in even one of Your mighty deeds (which are of the highest quality)?

וּמִי דוֹמֶה לָּךְ

You are the King over all

מֶלֶךְ

Who causes death and revival in many respects (such as sleep and awakening, poverty and wealth)

מֵמִית וּמְחַיֶּה

and, like the sprouting of a seed, You bring the Salvation (the Revival of the Dead)

וּמַצְמִיחַ יְשׁוּעָה

ON SHABBOS SHUVAH THE FOLLOWING IS ADDED:

Who is like You, who has as much mercy on his sons as You, the Merciful Father, have for us

מִי כָמוֹךָ אַב הָרַחֲמִים

(and) remembers His creatures, out of mercy, for life

זוֹכֵר יְצוּרָיו לְחַיִּים בְּרַחֲמִים

And (from the mighty deeds that we mentioned) we see that You are surely trusted to revive the dead

וְנֶאֱמָן אַתָּה לְהַחֲיוֹת מֵתִים

You are the Source of Blessing, Master of all

בָּרוּךְ אַתָּה יהוה

the Reviver of all the dead (from Adam until the time of the Revival). [2]

מְחַיֵּה הַמֵּתִים:

קדושת השם
Holiness of God

You, Yourself, are holy (different and separate from everything)

אַתָּה קָדוֹשׁ

and Your Name (which comes from Your many acts) reveals holiness

וְשִׁמְךָ קָדוֹשׁ

and the holy ones — Israel

וּקְדוֹשִׁים

constantly praise You, every day, forever

בְּכָל יוֹם יְהַלְלוּךָ סֶּלָה

You are the Source of Blessing, Master of all

בָּרוּךְ אַתָּה יהוה

the Almighty, Who is holier than all else

הָאֵל הַקָּדוֹשׁ.

ON SHABBOS SHUVAH THE FOLLOWING IS SAID *INSTEAD* OF THE LAST LINE ABOVE:

the King Who is holier than all else.

הַמֶּלֶךְ הַקָּדוֹשׁ.

---

2. Even though many bodies have decomposed over thousands of years, and some have been burned and their dust has been scattered, and others have drowned at sea, *Hashem* with His great might will recognize and recompose the bodies and return to them their original souls (*Yesod Veshoresh Ha'avodah*).

קְדוּשַׁת הַיּוֹם - שַׁבָּת שֶׁלֶעָתִיד לָבוֹא

Holiness of the Day–Shabbos of the World to Come[3]

You (Hashem) are the ultimate Oneness[4] — אַתָּה אֶחָד

and Your Name (which comes from Your many acts) reveals unity — וְשִׁמְךָ אֶחָד

and who from all the nations of the world is like Your nation Israel — וּמִי כְּעַמְּךָ יִשְׂרָאֵל

that is a unique and chosen nation on earth?[5] — גּוֹי אֶחָד בָּאָרֶץ

(You gave us Shabbos which is) the glory of greatness (since, like kings, we do not work on it) — תִּפְאֶרֶת גְּדֻלָּה

and it is the crown of salvation (for in the merit of keeping Shabbos the ultimate salvation will come) — וַעֲטֶרֶת יְשׁוּעָה

a day of rest for the body, and of holiness for the soul (for on Shabbos it is free of mundane pursuits) — יוֹם מְנוּחָה וּקְדֻשָּׁה

You have given to Your nation. — לְעַמְּךָ נָתָתָּ

---

3. We have mentioned (in note 3 of *Shacharis*) that the commentators say that the Shabbos *Minchah* corresponds to the Shabbos of the World to Come. Although the future is not mentioned explicitly, the reference is to what is prophesied by *Zechariah* (14:9): "on that day Hashem will be One and His name will be One," which means, as *Rashi* says there, that all the gentiles will then recognize that Hashem is One.

4. The *Rishonim* (*Tosafos Chagigah* 3b, *Tur O.C.* 292, and others) cite a *Midrash* that says that three testify on each other: Hashem, Israel and Shabbos. Hashem and Israel testify that Shabbos is the designated day of rest; Israel and Shabbos testify that Hashem is One; and Hashem and Shabbos testify that Israel is unique among the nations. This is the reason for the first few phrases of this *berachah*, for it is fitting for the One God to single out the unique nation on the special day of the week.

5. One should concentrate here to give a great thanks to Hashem for choosing us from amongst all the other nations. (*Yesod Veshoresh Ha'avodah*)

Abraham[6] rejoices in his heart

אַבְרָהָם יָגֵל

(and) Isaac even sings in joy

יִצְחָק יְרַנֵּן

that Jacob and his sons rest on Shabbos and keep it.

יַעֲקֹב וּבָנָיו יָנוּחוּ בוֹ

(Shabbos is) a rest that is kept out of love of Hashem and sincere beneficence

מְנוּחַת אַהֲבָה וּנְדָבָה

(and also) a rest that is kept in truth and faith (recognizing that Hashem created the world)

מְנוּחַת אֱמֶת וֶאֱמוּנָה

it is a rest of external peace and inner serenity

מְנוּחַת שָׁלוֹם וְשַׁלְוָה

and (a rest of) tranquility (on the present) and trust for the future (for any wars)

וְהַשְׁקֵט וָבֶטַח

(Shabbos is) a perfect rest (for its rest enables us to serve Hashem with all our abilities)

מְנוּחָה שְׁלֵמָה

(which is the kind of rest) that You desire (for You want us to reach spiritual perfection)[7]

שָׁאַתָּה רוֹצֶה בָּהּ

(and You want) Your children (Israel) to recognize and know clearly

יַכִּירוּ בָנֶיךָ וְיֵדְעוּ

---

6. *Kolbo* (Ch. 40) states that the reason the Patriarchs are mentioned in this prayer is because they were the first ones to make known Hashem's Oneness in the world, which is the theme of this *berachah*. He also quotes *R' Nosson* who says that we mention the Patriarchs because they all kept Shabbos

    The reason that only Jacob's sons are mentioned in regard to keeping Shabbos is explained by the *Shibolay Haleket* (Ch. 126) who quotes his brother *R' Binyomin:* the children of Abraham and Isaac were not given Shabbos (since *Yishmael* and the sons of *Keturah*, Abraham's other children; and Esau, Isaac's other child, did not go in their fathers' ways). Only Jacob's children, who all followed in his ways, were given the gift of Shabbos.

7. *R' Yehuda ben Yakar* writes that even though Shabbos is a "day of rest", one should **not** think that he may sleep and rest the entire day, and not devote any time to spiritual pursuits. This is not true "rest," and is not the intended way to spend the exalted day of Shabbos. Rather, the physical rest from work is meant to provide us with the opportunity to use all of our abilities to do *mitzvos* and serve Hashem.

that their rest is from You (not just for physical rest, but to learn Torah and recognize Hashem) כִּי מֵאִתְּךָ הִיא מְנוּחָתָם

and that through their rest וְעַל מְנוּחָתָם

they sanctify Your name. יַקְדִּישׁוּ אֶת שְׁמֶךָ.

The Master of all strength Who is able to do anything and Who takes care of us with Divine Providence **אֱלֹהֵינוּ**

and the God Who took care of our Fathers with Divine Providence וֵאלֹהֵי אֲבוֹתֵינוּ

let our rest be pleasant before You רְצֵה בִמְנוּחָתֵנוּ

make us holy from Above so that we should keep Your mitzvos properly קַדְּשֵׁנוּ בְּמִצְוֹתֶיךָ

and grant us Divine assistance that all of our occupation should be in Torah study וְתֵן חֶלְקֵנוּ בְּתוֹרָתֶךָ

bestow upon us good in a way that we will be satisfied with what we have (and not pursue our desires) שַׂבְּעֵנוּ מִטּוּבֶךָ

and cause us to rejoice through the salvation that You will bring us וְשַׂמְּחֵנוּ בִּישׁוּעָתֶךָ

and (we ask that You) purify our hearts so that we serve You sincerely (without other motives) וְטַהֵר לִבֵּנוּ לְעָבְדְּךָ בֶּאֱמֶת

and give us as an inheritance (the holiness that Shabbos inspires) וְהַנְחִילֵנוּ

Master of all, the Master of all strength Who is able to do anything and Who takes care of us with Divine Providence יהוה אֱלֹהֵינוּ

because of the love that You have for us (by giving us Shabbos) בְּאַהֲבָה

and because of the desire You have for us (that You want us to bring sacrifices even on Shabbos)	וּבְרָצוֹן
[give us as an inheritance] (the inspiration of) Shabbos that You made holy	שַׁבַּת קָדְשֶׁךָ
and (through this inspiration) You should cause Israel to have a complete rest on Shabbos	וְיָנוּחוּ בָם יִשְׂרָאֵל
for they sanctify Your Name (by keeping Shabbos)	מְקַדְּשֵׁי שְׁמֶךָ
You are the Source of Blessing, Master of all	בָּרוּךְ אַתָּה יהוה
Who made the Shabbos holier (than the other days — and gave it to us as a present).[8]	מְקַדֵּשׁ הַשַּׁבָּת.

עבודה
Return of the Temple Service

Be pleased[9]	רְצֵה
Master of all	יהוה
the Master of all strength, Who is able to do anything and Who takes care of us with Divine Providence	אֱלֹהֵינוּ

---

8. One should concentrate at this point on giving great praise and thanks to Hashem for this great gift of Shabbos, and he should give this thanks with great joy. (*Yesod Veshoresh Ha'avodah*)

9. Before this blessing one should instill in his heart love of all Jews, no matter what country or group they belong to, for we ask God here that He should be pleased with all of His nation, Israel (*Darchay Chayim*). [The saintly Chofetz Chaim wrote in *Ahavas Yisrael* (Ch. 2) that we pray constantly for the rebuilding of the Temple, but we don't contemplate the cause of its destruction, which was hatred for an unjustifiable reason. Therefore if we want the Temple to be rebuilt we first must rectify this sin and love all Jews.]

with Your nation, Israel (because they are praying for the rebuilding of the Temple)

בְּעַמְּךָ יִשְׂרָאֵל

and with their prayer (for the rebuilding of the Temple)

וּבִתְפִלָּתָם

and return the service of the Temple

וְהָשֵׁב אֶת הָעֲבוֹדָה

(even) to the Holy of Holies.

לִדְבִיר בֵּיתֶךָ

And the fire-offerings that they will bring

וְאִשֵּׁי יִשְׂרָאֵל

and the prayer of Israel (which is now in place of the offerings)

וּתְפִלָּתָם

because of Your love for the Jews

בְּאַהֲבָה

accept with desire

תְקַבֵּל בְּרָצוֹן

and help us that it should always be desirable

וּתְהִי לְרָצוֹן תָּמִיד

the service (whether offerings or prayers) of Israel, Your nation

עֲבוֹדַת יִשְׂרָאֵל עַמֶּךָ

ON *ROSH CHODESH* AND ON *CHOL HAMOED* THE FOLLOWING IS SAID:

The Master of all strength Who is able to do anything and Who takes care of us with Divine Providence

אֱלֹהֵינוּ

and the God who took care of our Fathers with Divine Providence,

וֵאלֹהֵי אֲבוֹתֵינוּ

may our remembrance and consideration go up

יַעֲלֶה

and come

וְיָבֹא

and reach	וְיַגִּיעַ
and be seen in a good way	וְיֵרָאֶה
and be accepted with desire	וְיֵרָצֶה
and be heard well	וְיִשָּׁמַע
and be considered	וְיִפָּקֵד
and be remembered forever	וְיִזָּכֵר
our remembrance, i.e., our special relationship with You	זִכְרוֹנֵנוּ
and Your special consideration to do good for us	וּפִקְדוֹנֵנוּ
and the remembrance of the covenants You made with our Fathers	וְזִכְרוֹן אֲבוֹתֵינוּ
and the remembrance of the promise to bring *Mashiach*, a descendant of David Your servant	וְזִכְרוֹן מָשִׁיחַ בֶּן דָּוִד עַבְדֶּךָ
and the remembrance of Jerusalem, the city of Your Holiness, which is now in ruins	וְזִכְרוֹן יְרוּשָׁלַיִם עִיר קָדְשֶׁךָ
and the remembrance of Your nation, the House of Israel, which is now in exile	וְזִכְרוֹן כָּל עַמְּךָ בֵּית יִשְׂרָאֵל
(may all of these remembrances) come before You	לְפָנֶיךָ
for salvation (for all of Israel)	לִפְלֵיטָה
for good (for all of Israel)	לְטוֹבָה
to find favor in Your eyes and in everyone's eyes	לְחֵן
and to grant us our requests (even though we are not deserving)	וּלְחֶסֶד
and for mercy (not punishing us according to our wrongdoings)	וּלְרַחֲמִים
and for life (for all of Israel)	וּלְחַיִּים

and for peace (for all of Israel) — וּלְשָׁלוֹם

on this day of *Rosh Chodesh* — **בְּיוֹם רֹאשׁ הַחֹדֶשׁ הַזֶּה** On *Rosh Chodesh*

on this day of the Festival of *Matzos* — **בְּיוֹם חַג הַמַּצוֹת הַזֶּה** On *Chol Hamoed Pesach*

on this day of the Festival of *Succos* — **בְּיוֹם חַג הַסֻּכּוֹת הַזֶּה** On *Chol Hamoed Succos*

Remember us, Master of all — זָכְרֵנוּ יהוה

the Master of all strength, Who is able to do anything and Who takes care of us with Divine Providence — אֱלֹהֵינוּ

[remember us] on this day to give everyone whatever is good for him — בּוֹ לְטוֹבָה

and consider us on this day for prosperity and success — וּפָקְדֵנוּ בוֹ לִבְרָכָה

and save us on this day so that we will merit life — וְהוֹשִׁיעֵנוּ בוֹ לְחַיִּים

and with Your promise to save us and to have mercy on us — וּבִדְבַר יְשׁוּעָה וְרַחֲמִים

have mercy on us because You are our Creator, and favor us (with salvation) — חוּס וְחָנֵּנוּ

and have mercy on us because of our lowly nature and save us, even though we are undeserving — וְרַחֵם עָלֵינוּ וְהוֹשִׁיעֵנוּ

because our eyes are looking to You in hope — כִּי אֵלֶיךָ עֵינֵינוּ

because You are the Almighty King over all — כִּי אֵל מֶלֶךְ

and You are gracious and merciful (even to the undeserving). — חַנּוּן וְרַחוּם אָתָּה.

and let us merit to see (the *Shechinah* — Divine Presence) with our own eyes (i.e., soon, in our days) — וְתֶחֱזֶינָה עֵינֵינוּ

when You return Your Presence to the Temple (even if it is) in mercy (and not through our merits) — בְּשׁוּבְךָ לְצִיּוֹן בְּרַחֲמִים

You are the Source of Blessing, Master of all — בָּרוּךְ אַתָּה יהוה

Who will return His Divine Presence to the Temple. — הַמַּחֲזִיר שְׁכִינָתוֹ לְצִיּוֹן.

הודאה
Thanking God[10]

We give thanks to You, acknowledging	**מוֹדִים** אֲנַחְנוּ לָךְ
that You are the Master of all	שָׁאַתָּה הוּא יהוה
the Master of all strength, Who is able to do anything and Who takes care of us with Divine Providence	אֱלֹהֵינוּ
and the God Who took care of our Fathers with Divine Providence	וֵאלֹהֵי אֲבוֹתֵינוּ
(and that You will continue to take care of us) forever	לְעוֹלָם וָעֶד
[You are] the Rock — Creator and Sustainer — of our lives	צוּר חַיֵּינוּ
[and You are] the Protector Who saves us from all troubles	מָגֵן יִשְׁעֵנוּ
You are the One [Who keeps us alive and saves us] in every generation.	אַתָּה הוּא לְדוֹר וָדוֹר
We will always express our thanks to You	נוֹדֶה לְּךָ
and we will tell Your praise to others	וּנְסַפֵּר תְּהִלָּתֶךָ
for our lives — each breath — that is given over into Your hand	עַל חַיֵּינוּ הַמְּסוּרִים בְּיָדֶךָ
and for our souls that are entrusted to You (while we sleep)	וְעַל נִשְׁמוֹתֵינוּ הַפְּקוּדוֹת לָךְ

---

10. The *Bais Elokim* explains that the reason we bow at the beginning and end of this *berachah* is to show humility, recognizing our unworthiness for *Hashem*'s special care, and realizing that all our lives and all goodness come from Him.

and for the hidden miracles that You do for us every day	וְעַל נִסֶּיךָ שֶׁבְּכָל יוֹם עִמָּנוּ
and for Your wonders of "nature" (which You renew constantly)	וְעַל נִפְלְאוֹתֶיךָ
and for Your favors (that You do for us constantly)	וְטוֹבוֹתֶיךָ
that You do in all parts of the day	שֶׁבְּכָל עֵת
in the evening, morning, and afternoon.	עֶרֶב וָבֹקֶר וְצָהֳרָיִם
You are the ultimate Good One	הַטּוֹב
for Your mercy has never finished — for You withhold punishment from those deserving it	כִּי לֹא כָלוּ רַחֲמֶיךָ
and You are the ultimate Merciful One (Who not only withholds punishment, but...)	וְהַמְרַחֵם
Whose kindness never ends — for You even give these undeserving people additional kindnesses	כִּי לֹא תַמּוּ חֲסָדֶיךָ
we have always put our hope in You.	מֵעוֹלָם קִוִּינוּ לָךְ

ON CHANUKAH AND PURIM ONE ADDS עַל הַנִּסִים FOUND ON P. 90.

And for all of these wonders and favors that You do for us constantly	וְעַל כֻּלָּם
[Your Name] should be praised with the recognition that You are the Source of all Blessing	יִתְבָּרַךְ
and may Your Name (which represents Your acts) be exalted through the recognition of Your greatness	וְיִתְרוֹמַם שִׁמְךָ

since You are our King (Who takes care of us especially) [we desire that Your Name be praised and exalted]

מַלְכֵּנוּ

constantly, every day

תָּמִיד

forever and ever.

לְעוֹלָם וָעֶד.

And inscribe for a good life (i.e., life that will be good for earning the World to Come)

וּכְתוֹב לְחַיִּים טוֹבִים

all the children of Your covenant

כָּל בְּנֵי בְרִיתֶךָ

And all the living (those who will come back to life by the Revival of the Dead)

וְכֹל הַחַיִּים

will thank You constantly forever

יוֹדוּךָ סֶּלָה

and they will praise Your Name (which comes from Your deeds) truthfully, without any other motive

וִיהַלְלוּ אֶת שִׁמְךָ בֶּאֱמֶת

the Almighty

הָאֵל

Who saves us in all our troubles

יְשׁוּעָתֵנוּ

and Who helps us to succeed

וְעֶזְרָתֵנוּ

constantly, forever

סֶלָה

You are the Source of Blessing, Master of all

בָּרוּךְ אַתָּה יהוה

Whose Name is "The Good One" (for You are the ultimate good)

הַטּוֹב שִׁמְךָ

and to You alone is it fitting to give thanks (because You are the cause of all goodness).

וּלְךָ נָאֶה לְהוֹדוֹת.

שלום
Peace[11]

THE CUSTOM OF MOST IS TO SAY THE FOLLOWING, HOWEVER SOME SAY שים שלום (BELOW):

שָׁלוֹם רָב An abundant peace (which includes peace of mind, peace in one's house, peace between Jews, and peace in one's country)

עַל יִשְׂרָאֵל עַמְּךָ תָּשִׂים לְעוֹלָם May You place upon Israel, Your nation, forever

כִּי אַתָּה הוּא מֶלֶךְ for You are the King over all

אָדוֹן לְכָל הַשָּׁלוֹם (and) the Master of all forms of peace (You can make peace in any situation).

CONTINUE AT וטוב בעיניך ON PAGE 86

SOME SAY THE FOLLOWING:

שִׂים שָׁלוֹם Grant peace (which includes peace of mind, peace in one's house, peace between Jews, and peace in the country)

טוֹבָה (and grant what is) good for each person

וּבְרָכָה and (grant) prosperity and success

חֵן (and) let us find favor in Your eyes and thereby find favor in the eyes of all who see us

וָחֶסֶד and grant our requests (even though we are not deserving)

וְרַחֲמִים and have mercy on us (not to punish us according to our wrongdoings)

עָלֵינוּ on those of us here (praying together)

וְעַל כָּל יִשְׂרָאֵל עַמֶּךָ and on all of Israel, Your nation.

---

11. The last *mishnah* states that God found no adequate vehicle for Israel's blessing other than peace. The Sages tell us (*Vayikra Rabbah* 9:9) that peace is so great that

Since You are our Father, give us an abundance of goodness and success   בָּרְכֵנוּ אָבִינוּ

all of us like one (equally)   כֻּלָּנוּ כְּאֶחָד

with the "light of Your face" (which is a symbol of Your great love)   בְּאוֹר פָּנֶיךָ

because, as we already know from the Revelation at Sinai, that with the "light of Your face" come great things: כִּי בְאוֹר פָּנֶיךָ

You gave to us as a present (not because we were deserving),   נָתַתָּ לָּנוּ

Master of all   יהוה

the Master of all strength, Who is able to do anything and Who takes care of us with Divine Providence,   אֱלֹהֵינוּ

the Torah that teaches us how to live   תּוֹרַת חַיִּים

and (through it) the love of doing kindness   וְאַהֲבַת חֶסֶד

and (You gave us with the Torah more opportunities for) reward in the World to Come (by fulfilling the many *mitzvos*)   וּצְדָקָה

and (as reward for keeping the Torah You give us also) an abundance of goodness and success (in this world)   וּבְרָכָה

and (in the merit of keeping the Torah You give us) special mercy   וְרַחֲמִים

and (as a reward for keeping the Torah You give us) a long, healthy life   וְחַיִּים

---

it comes at the end of all prayers. As the *Seder Hayom* [R' Moshe ben Yehuda Machir (16th cent.)] writes, "Peace encompasses everything and through peace we will merit everything." Therefore, one should concentrate especially on this all-encompassing final *berachah*.

and (through the Torah we have) peace of body and mind   וְשָׁלוֹם
(because all the ways of the Torah are peaceful)

EVERYONE CONTINUES HERE

And it should be good in Your eyes   וְטוֹב בְּעֵינֶיךָ

to give an abundance of goodness and success to   לְבָרֵךְ אֶת עַמְּךָ יִשְׂרָאֵל
Your nation, Israel

in all parts of the day   בְּכָל עֵת

and in all hours of each part of the day   וּבְכָל שָׁעָה

with Your peace (which is a complete peace).   בִּשְׁלוֹמֶךָ.

ON SHABBOS SHUVAH THE FOLLOWING IS ADDED:

In the book of life (of ...)   בְּסֵפֶר חַיִּים

of abundant goodness and success   בְּרָכָה

and peace between a man and his friend   וְשָׁלוֹם

and a good (ample and easy) livelihood   וּפַרְנָסָה טוֹבָה

may we be remembered   נִזָּכֵר

and may we be inscribed before You   וְנִכָּתֵב לְפָנֶיךָ

we (who are standing together praying)   אֲנַחְנוּ

and all of Your nation, Israel   וְכָל עַמְּךָ בֵּית יִשְׂרָאֵל

(let us be remembered and inscribed) for a truly good life   לְחַיִּים טוֹבִים
(i.e., a life that will enable us to earn the World to Come)

and for peace within ourselves (that we should be   וּלְשָׁלוֹם
satisfied with the materialistic things that we have)

SOME SAY THE FOLLOWING CONCLUSION ON SHABBOS SHUVAH
INSTEAD OF THE REGULAR CONCLUSION TO THE BLESSING

(You are the Source of Blessing, Master of all   (בָּרוּךְ אַתָּה יהוה

Who makes peace among all.)	עוֹשֶׂה הַשָּׁלוֹם.)
You are the Source of Blessing, Master of all	בָּרוּךְ אַתָּה יהוה
Who gives an abundance of goodness and success to His nation, Israel, with peace.	הַמְבָרֵךְ אֶת עַמּוֹ יִשְׂרָאֵל בַּשָּׁלוֹם.

תחנונים
Personal Requests

The Master of all strength Who is able to do anything and Who takes care of me with Divine Providence	אֱלֹהַי
help me to guard my tongue from speaking bad about others (*Lashon Hora*)	נְצוֹר לְשׁוֹנִי מֵרָע
and [help me to guard] my lips from speaking deceit or falsehood	וּשְׂפָתַי מִדַּבֵּר מִרְמָה
and help me so that my soul should be silent (that even in thought I should not get angry) at those who curse me	וְלִמְקַלְלַי נַפְשִׁי תִדֹּם
and help me so that my soul should be like dust (very humble) before everyone (and not mind insults).	וְנַפְשִׁי כֶּעָפָר לַכֹּל תִּהְיֶה
Open up my heart so that it should be receptive and understand Your Torah	פְּתַח לִבִּי בְּתוֹרָתֶךָ
and help my soul eagerly pursue Your *mitzvos*	וּבְמִצְוֹתֶיךָ תִּרְדּוֹף נַפְשִׁי
and all those who want to harm me (whether in mundane matters or spiritual matters, i.e., to cause me to sin)	וְכֹל הַחוֹשְׁבִים עָלַי רָעָה
quickly annul their plan	מְהֵרָה הָפֵר עֲצָתָם

and ruin their thought (even before they make plans). וְקַלְקֵל מַחֲשַׁבְתָּם

Act (take us out of exile) for the sake of Your Name, עֲשֵׂה לְמַעַן שְׁמֶךְ
which is desecrated now among the gentiles

act (take us out of exile) for the sake of Your right עֲשֵׂה לְמַעַן יְמִינֶךְ
hand, which You have now withdrawn in our exile

act (take us out of exile) for the sake of Your עֲשֵׂה לְמַעַן קְדֻשָׁתֶךְ
Holiness (so that all will know that You lead us
with holiness)

act (take us out of exile) for the sake of Your עֲשֵׂה לְמַעַן תּוֹרָתֶךְ
Torah (so the Torah can be studied properly
and completely)

and in order that Your dear ones, Israel, לְמַעַן יֵחָלְצוּן יְדִידֶיךָ
should be released from all troubles

save them with (the wonders and miracles that הוֹשִׁיעָה יְמִינְךָ
are attributed to) Your right hand

and answer (even) me in this prayer. וַעֲנֵנִי.

Let the words of my prayer be desirable to You[12] יִהְיוּ לְרָצוֹן אִמְרֵי פִי

and also the thoughts of my heart which I וְהֶגְיוֹן לִבִּי לְפָנֶיךָ
cannot express [should be desirable] before You

Master of all יהוה

My Rock, Whom I rely on for all my requests צוּרִי

and Who will be my Redeemer. וְגוֹאֲלִי.

ONE SHOULD BOW AND GO BACK 3 STEPS LIKE A SERVANT DEPARTING FROM HIS MASTER

---

12. *Seder Hayom* (quoted also in *Mishnah Berurah* 122:8) writes that one should say
this verse with great concentration, for it will help a great deal that his prayers
should not go unanswered.

The One Who makes peace in Heaven (among the angels)	**עֹשֶׂה שָׁלוֹם** בִּמְרוֹמָיו
may He make peace (for those on earth, who are naturally quarrelsome)	הוּא יַעֲשֶׂה שָׁלוֹם
on those of us here (praying together)	עָלֵינוּ
and on all of Israel	וְעַל כָּל יִשְׂרָאֵל
and (you, the angels who escort me,) agree to my prayer, and say Amen!	וְאִמְרוּ אָמֵן.
May it be Your desire	**יְהִי רָצוֹן** מִלְּפָנֶיךָ
Master of all	יהוה
the Master of all strength, Who is able to do anything and Who takes care of us with Divine Providence	אֱלֹהֵינוּ
and the God Who took care of our Fathers with Divine Providence	וֵאלֹהֵי אֲבוֹתֵינוּ
that You should rebuild the Temple (so that we will be able to do the ultimate *avodah* - service to You)	שֶׁיִּבָּנֶה בֵּית הַמִּקְדָּשׁ
quickly and in our lifetime	בִּמְהֵרָה בְיָמֵינוּ
and help us so that all our toil should be in learning Your Torah.	וְתֵן חֶלְקֵנוּ בְּתוֹרָתֶךָ.
And there, in the Temple, we will bring offerings (the ultimate service) with reverence	וְשָׁם נַעֲבָדְךָ בְּיִרְאָה
as [they brought offerings and served in reverence] in the earlier days (of Moshe)	כִּימֵי עוֹלָם
and as they did in the previous years (of Shlomo *Hamelech*).	וּכְשָׁנִים קַדְמוֹנִיּוֹת.
And then, it will be pleasing to the Master of all	וְעָרְבָה לַיהוה
the offerings that will be brought in the Temple (which is in the portion of Yehudah in Jerusalem)	מִנְחַת יְהוּדָה וִירוּשָׁלָיִם
as [the offerings were pleasing] in the earlier days (of Moshe)	כִּימֵי עוֹלָם
and as they were in the previous years (of Shlomo *Hamelech*).	וּכְשָׁנִים קַדְמוֹנִיּוֹת.

On Chanukah and Purim say:

עַל הַנִּסִּים, וְעַל הַפֻּרְקָן, וְעַל הַגְּבוּרוֹת, וְעַל הַתְּשׁוּעוֹת, וְעַל הַמִּלְחָמוֹת, שֶׁעָשִׂיתָ לַאֲבוֹתֵינוּ בַּיָּמִים הָהֵם בַּזְּמַן הַזֶּה.

On Chanukah say:

בִּימֵי מַתִּתְיָהוּ בֶּן יוֹחָנָן כֹּהֵן גָּדוֹל, חַשְׁמוֹנַאי וּבָנָיו, כְּשֶׁעָמְדָה מַלְכוּת יָוָן הָרְשָׁעָה עַל עַמְּךָ יִשְׂרָאֵל, לְהַשְׁכִּיחָם תּוֹרָתֶךָ, וּלְהַעֲבִירָם מֵחֻקֵּי רְצוֹנֶךָ, וְאַתָּה בְּרַחֲמֶיךָ הָרַבִּים עָמַדְתָּ לָהֶם בְּעֵת צָרָתָם, רַבְתָּ אֶת רִיבָם, דַּנְתָּ אֶת דִּינָם, נָקַמְתָּ אֶת נִקְמָתָם, מָסַרְתָּ גִבּוֹרִים בְּיַד חַלָּשִׁים, וְרַבִּים בְּיַד מְעַטִּים, וּטְמֵאִים בְּיַד טְהוֹרִים, וּרְשָׁעִים בְּיַד צַדִּיקִים, וְזֵדִים בְּיַד עוֹסְקֵי תוֹרָתֶךָ. וּלְךָ עָשִׂיתָ שֵׁם גָּדוֹל וְקָדוֹשׁ בְּעוֹלָמֶךָ, וּלְעַמְּךָ יִשְׂרָאֵל עָשִׂיתָ תְּשׁוּעָה גְדוֹלָה וּפֻרְקָן כְּהַיּוֹם הַזֶּה. וְאַחַר כֵּן בָּאוּ בָנֶיךָ לִדְבִיר בֵּיתֶךָ, וּפִנּוּ אֶת הֵיכָלֶךָ, וְטִהֲרוּ אֶת מִקְדָּשֶׁךָ, וְהִדְלִיקוּ נֵרוֹת בְּחַצְרוֹת קָדְשֶׁךָ, וְקָבְעוּ שְׁמוֹנַת יְמֵי חֲנֻכָּה אֵלּוּ, לְהוֹדוֹת וּלְהַלֵּל לְשִׁמְךָ הַגָּדוֹל. וְעל כולם...

On Purim say:

בִּימֵי מָרְדְּכַי וְאֶסְתֵּר בְּשׁוּשַׁן הַבִּירָה, כְּשֶׁעָמַד עֲלֵיהֶם הָמָן הָרָשָׁע, בִּקֵּשׁ לְהַשְׁמִיד, לַהֲרֹג וּלְאַבֵּד אֶת כָּל הַיְּהוּדִים, מִנַּעַר וְעַד זָקֵן, טַף וְנָשִׁים, בְּיוֹם אֶחָד בִּשְׁלשָׁה עָשָׂר לְחֹדֶשׁ שְׁנֵים עָשָׂר, הוּא חֹדֶשׁ אֲדָר, וּשְׁלָלָם לָבוֹז. וְאַתָּה בְּרַחֲמֶיךָ הָרַבִּים הֵפַרְתָּ אֶת עֲצָתוֹ, וְקִלְקַלְתָּ אֶת מַחֲשַׁבְתּוֹ, וַהֲשֵׁבוֹתָ לּוֹ גְּמוּלוֹ בְּרֹאשׁוֹ, וְתָלוּ אוֹתוֹ וְאֶת בָּנָיו עַל הָעֵץ. וְעל כולם...

Excerpts from

PRACTICAL HALACHOS
— OF —
SHABBOS

This book received the Haskamos of:
Horav Hagaon **R' Shmuel Kamenetsky** shlita (Rosh Yeshiva of Philadelphia Yeshiva)
Horav Hagaon **R' Yaakov Perlow** shlita (Noveminsker Rebbe)
Horav Hagaon **R' Reuven Feinstein** shlita (Rosh Yeshiva of Yeshiva of Staten Island)

As in the Hebrew edition, I thought it would be beneficial to include some laws of Shabbos as an addendum. I am including here excerpts from my book **Practical Halachos of Shabbos** (*Torah Umesorah Publications*). I have chosen primarily laws concerning food preparation (the first 11 *melachos*) and added another chapter with examples of the laws from the remaining Lessons in that work, concerning the other *melachos*. These are merely *examples* of practical relevant laws that everyone must know to keep Shabbos. There are **many more** laws which I have not included (even from the first 11 *melachos*), since they are beyond the scope of this work. It is suggested that the reader look in the **Practical Halachos of Shabbos** for many other relevant laws, all written in an interesting, easy-to-understand format.

The truth, however, is that even that work is not a complete guide to the laws of Shabbos, and everyone is encouraged to learn **all** the laws of Shabbos in order to properly keep Shabbos. An excellent work that covers all of the laws of Shabbos in a practical way is *Shemirath Shabbath* (*Feldheim Publishers*).

List of Abbreviations:

O.C. = Shulchan Aruch **O**rach **C**haim

M.B. = **M**ishnah **B**erurah

I.M. = **I**gros **M**oshe

H.S. = **H**alachos of **S**habbos (by R' Shimon Eider)

S.S.K. = **S**hmiras **S**habbos **K**ehilchasa (Shemirath Shabbath)

S.H. = **S**habbos **H**ome (by R' Simcha Bunim Cohen)

Table of Contents

Chapter 1
The Greatness of Keeping Shabbos

Every Jew who keeps Shabbos, which is the special sign between us and Hashem, is testifying that He created the world in six days and rested on Shabbos.

What does it mean to "keep Shabbos"? It says in the Ten Commandments (*Devarim* 5:12-14):

"שָׁמוֹר אֶת יוֹם הַשַׁבָּת לְקַדְּשׁוֹ ... לֹא תַעֲשֶׂה כָל מְלָאכָה"

"You should keep the day of Shabbos to make it holy ...
you should not do any work."

Although the Torah does not state exactly what work is forbidden, the *Mishnah* (*Shabbos* 7:2) says that there are 39 *Avos Melachos*, Main Categories of Work, which are forbidden on Shabbos. Many of these categories have sub-categories (called *Toldos*) which are equally forbidden (*Rambam, Hilchos Shabbos* 7:7); for example, watering plants is a sub-category of planting (ibid. 8:2). Therefore, there are many more than 39 activities which the Torah prohibits on Shabbos.*

In addition to these biblical prohibitions, *Chazal* (the Sages from the time of the *Mishnayos* and *Gemara* [from 1st - 5th cent. C.E.]) enacted many laws to prevent us from transgressing any of the *melachos*, as well as some restrictions to preserve the spirit of Shabbos.

Many of the questions that arise today, especially in modern times, were not discussed by the Sages because they did not exist in those times; for example, those regarding electricity. These questions were dealt with by the great sages of each generation who, based on their tremendous Torah knowledge, decided what the *halachah* (Jewish law) concerning these things should be.**

Every man and woman is **obligated to keep all of these laws, because the Torah commanded us to** listen to whatever the Sages of our generation tell us (*Devarim* 17:11; see *Chinuch, Mitzvos* 495 and 496).

---

* It should be noted that one who desecrates Shabbos by intentionally doing any of the things that the Torah forbids receives the same death sentence as an idol worshiper! And just as one who worships idols is considered as if he had transgressed the entire Torah, so, too, one who desecrates Shabbos. On the other hand, **keeping Shabbos** is equal to keeping the entire Torah (*Rashi, Bamidbar* 15:41).

** Two of the great sages of the previous generation who dealt with many of the modern questions of their time were: *Horav Hagaon* **Rav Moshe Feinstein** *zt"l* (1895-1986) and *Horav Hagaon* **Rav Shlomo Zalman Auerbach** *zt"l* (1910-1995).

Chapter 2

The first four of the 39 *Melachos* are

Plowing or anything done to improve land - חוֹרֵשׁ
Planting or anything done to help plants grow - זוֹרֵעַ
Harvesting or detaching a plant from the ground - קוֹצֵר
Gathering detached plants into piles - מְעַמֵּר

Here are a few practical applications for these *melachos*:

1) One may not smooth out the ground by moving dirt or a stone to make it flat (M.B. end of Ch. 336).

2) One may not play soccer or marbles outside [because the Sages were afraid that one may smooth out the ground to play*] (O.C. 338:5 and M.B. 308:158).

3) Since it is forbidden to plant, if one eats watermelon outside he must be careful not to drop any pits on the ground (O.C. 336:4).

4) One must be careful when opening a *succah* covering, or tilting a chair that has water on it, not to roll it up or tilt it in a way that the water will go directly on the grass (H.S. p. 59 par. 6).

5) One may not open a window shade so that the sunlight will shine on a plant, nor open a window in order to benefit a plant (H.S. p. 64).

6) It is forbidden to detach, in any way, anything that grew on the ground, whether a food or a plant, from its attachment to the ground (*Eglay Tal, Kotzair* 1). This includes even pulling off a leaf.

7) If it gets too hot, one may not put his jacket or hat on a tree nor take anything off a tree, even if it was put there before Shabbos (*Ramoh* 336:1; M.B. 3).

8) The Sages said that it is forbidden to smell a fruit that is growing on a tree for fear one will be tempted to pull it off to eat [however, one may smell a flower or plant still attached to the ground] (O.C. 336:10).

9) It is forbidden to climb a tree or use a tree on Shabbos. Therefore, you may not lean all your weight on a tree to tie your shoe (O.C. 336:1 and M.B. 2; and H.S. p. 74).

10) The laws of מעמר apply only to things that grew on the ground, so there is no problem with cleaning up toys that are all over the room [provided you don't sort them out] (M.B. 340:37).

---

* It should be noted that playing ball is not a *Shabbosdik* activity. The *Midrash* (*Eichah* 2:4) states that an entire city was destroyed in the time of the *Bais Hamikdosh* because the people played ball on Shabbos [see also *M.B.* 518:9].

Chapter 3

The next three *melachos* which we will discuss are:

Threshing (separating food from its non-edible covering)- דָּשׁ

Grinding substances into very small particles - טוֹחֵן

Kneading or combining small particles into one mass - לָשׁ

These *melachos* are very applicable for we do them throughout the week. Here are some examples of what is forbidden on Shabbos:

1) One may not use a sponge on Shabbos [because he will squeeze the water out - a *Toldah* (sub-category) of דשׁ] (O.C. 320:17). So too, one may not use wet baby-wipes [rather one should clean the baby by pouring water onto the soiled area and using tissues or dried out baby wipes] (*Children in Halachah* p. 205-208; see similarly, H.S. p.105 note 176 in the name of R' Moshe Feinstein *zt"l*).

2) One may not squeeze any fruit that is normally squeezed for juice. Therefore, you may not squeeze out a grapefruit-half to get out the juice [but you may eat a grapefruit-half with a spoon even though some juice might be squeezed out while taking the fruit, as long as your intention is not for the juice] (O.C. 320:1 and S.S.K. 5:12).

3) Anything that grows on the ground may not be cut into tiny pieces. Therefore, you may not cut an onion into tiny pieces (dicing) [but you may cut it into small pieces that are a little larger than you usually cut it, preferably right before the meal] (M.B. 321:45).

4) There are two main exceptions concerning the prohibition of grinding:

   a) foods that do not grow on the ground do not have a prohibition of טוחן: therefore, one may cut meat or cheese into tiny pieces, but not with a specialized grinding utensil, like a grinder or grater (O.C. 321:9 and 10).

   b) there is no prohibition of grinding something that was already ground: therefore, one may crumble *challah* or a cookie [since these are made from flour that was already ground], but not with a specialized grinding utensil (*Ramoh* 321:12 and M.B. 321:30).

5) One may not take Tylenol or any other pain reliever for a regular headache [because the Sages, out of concern that someone might grind medicine, made a decree that no medicines could be taken,

except if one is really sick, for example, he has to lie down to feel better] (S.S.K. 34:6).

6) Current-day baby cereals, which are fine powders that turn into a thick mixture upon adding water (like Beech-nut Instant Cereal), may not be made on Shabbos in the normal way. One can make it by adding a **large** amount of liquid (so that it will not solidify even after mixing it), and then, only under the following conditions:

a) the ingredients must be **put into the bowl in the reverse order** (that is, if one usually puts in the powder first, then on Shabbos the water must be put in first),

and

b) it must be **stirred in an unusual manner**, that is, either with one's finger, or with the handle of a utensil, or by shaking the bowl, or crisscrossing with a spoon [but the spoon should be lifted out of the mixture with each change of direction] (*Shabbos Kitchen* p. 157 and *Children in Halachah* p. 100).

Chapter 4

Selecting or sorting a mixture - בּוֹרֵר

Of all the melachos, the Mishnah Berurah *writes that* **Borer** *is so commonly transgressed because of people's lack of knowledge of its many halachos* (Mishnah Berurah, introduction to Hilchos Shabbos).

There are actually three *melachos* that are very similar and are collectively referred to as *Borer*.

Selecting with wind - זוֹרֶה
Selecting by hand - בּוֹרֵר
Selecting with a utensil - מְרַקֵּד

The following illustrates the complexity of this *melachah*:

Question: How can two people do the identical action on Shabbos, one doing nothing wrong while the other is doing a *melachah*, that is, he is desecrating Shabbos ?

Answer: There are many cases involving *Borer* where this is so!

Let's just give two examples:

1) Reuven and Shimon are sitting down sharing a bowl of mixed nuts. **They both take out cashews.** Reuven likes cashews and wants to eat them, so he has done nothing wrong. But Shimon wants the rest of the nuts cashew-free because he doesn't like cashews, so by taking out the cashews he has done *Borer* !

> **Reason:** One is permitted to separate a mixture by taking what he **wants** and leaving what he doesn't want, but he may <u>not</u> take out what he doesn't want and leave the rest there.

2) Rochel and Leah are both setting up their Shabbos tables in their respective houses. **They both are separating knives from the mixed silverware.** Rochel is setting up to eat immediately after the table is set, so she has done nothing wrong. Leah, however, is setting up to eat after she comes home from shul, and has therefore done *Borer.*

> **Reason:** One is only allowed to remove the good, or what she wants, for **immediate** use. If she takes the "good" but it is not for immediate use, as in this case, where she went to *shul* first, it is <u>forbidden by the Torah</u>.

From these examples one should see how important it is to know the laws of *Borer* **thoroughly**. Since *Borer* applies to both foods and non-foods (like clothes, dishes, *sefarim*, etc.) it presents problems so frequently that situations involving it are impossible to avoid — every Shabbos. Therefore, it is **the most difficult *melacha* to avoid**.

Although *Borer* applies to almost any mixture, there are ways that most separating can be done **permissibly**.

Here are the general rules:

IF <u>ALL THREE</u> OF THE FOLLOWING CONDITIONS ARE MET, THEN YOU <u>MAY</u> SELECT FROM A MIXTURE:

1) אוכל מתוך פסולת - To separate **what you want** (אוכל) from what you don't want (פסולת), for example, to take only good grapes from a cluster of good and rotting grapes (O.C. 319:1 and S.S.K. 3:22). [EXCEPTIONS: When the food is in your mouth, you can take out just the unwanted matter, like a fish bone (*I.M. O.C. IV 74 Borer 7* and S.S.K. 3:11). Also, when the entire food is covered with what you don't want, such as an orange in its peel, then removing the peel is permitted *for immediate use* (O.C. 321:19 and S.S.K. 3:29)].

2) ביד - To separate it **with your hand**, not a utensil. This forbids using not only a specialized utensil (like a sieve), but even an ordinary utensil (like a fork), to assist in the selecting [unless the utensil is considered an extension of your hand, that is, when the utensil is used only as a convenience (so as not to get your hand dirty) but not aiding in the actual *Borer* (e.g. using your fork to take chicken off the bone, which could be done without a utensil and is therefore permissible) (*I.M. O.C.I* 124; S.S.K. 3:45)] (O.C. 319:1).

3) לאלתר - To separate it **for immediate use** [or, prior to a meal, the amount of time it takes to prepare that meal, without stopping for anything that is not preparation (*I.M. O.C. IV 74 Borer 13*)] (O.C. 319:1).

Here are some practical *halachos* that result from the three conditions for selecting:

1) You must separate **what you want** from what you don't want.

    a) removing even a little unwanted matter from a mixture is forbidden by the Torah*, even if you leave some of it in (O.C. 319:4 and S.S.K. 3:10).

---

* This refers to pieces of unwanted matter that are mixed into food; for example, dirt in

b) it is forbidden to remove something perfectly edible if you don't want it now, like onions from a salad (O.C. 319:3 and M.B. 12; and S.S.K.. 3:23).

2) You must separate it **with your hand**, not a utensil.

a) you cannot use a perforated or slotted spoon to take meat out of soup [allowing the soup to run out], or to take coleslaw [letting the juice run out] (S.S.K. 3:54 and so I heard from Rav Moshe Feinstein *zt"l*).

b) you may not use a pot lid to hold back the noodles or vegetables and just pour out the soup you want [but if you also let some noodles or vegetables out, it's permissible] (H.S. p. 166).

3) You may only separate it **for immediate use.**

a) you may not sort out different meats or cookies on a tray after a *kiddush* to put away (Shabbos Kitchen p. 116), nor may you sort out toys that are mixed together to put them away (S.S.K. 3:83).

b) you may not select clothes on Friday night for Shabbos morning (H.S. p. 181).

Here are some more *Halachos* concerning *Borer*:

1) Blowing a piece of dirt out of food is a biblical prohibition because of the *melacha* of *Zoreh* (Kitzur Hilchos Shabbos, *Zoreh*).

2) A cluster of grapes that has dirt mixed in it may not be soaked in a bowl for cleaning even to eat right away (O.C. 319:8 and M.B. 29). [Some say, however, that you may rinse them under a running faucet for immediate use. (I.M. *O.C. I 125*; see *Piskay Teshuvos* 319:10 for all the opinions).] But to wash off fruits just for hygienic reasons is permissible according to all (S.S.K. 3:21).

3) You may not sort out a pile of silverware, even one at a time at random, to put away [however, if silverware is wet you may pick up one piece at a time to dry it and then put it into its compartment] (S.S.K. 3:78).

---

a cluster of grapes. Removing even one piece of dirt is forbidden even though other pieces of dirt will remain there.

However, one **may** remove the unwanted matter together with some of the surrounding good; for example, if an insect fell into soup one may take it out with some soup, or, likewise, one may cut away a sliver of meat together with the fat (M.B. 319:62).

Chapter 5

The next *melacha* is one of the most important to learn, because of its many applications and the complexity of its *halachos*.

Cooking or Baking (including any way - בִּשׁוּל / אוֹפֶה of changing the quality of a substance with heat)

Let's give some examples of what is forbidden on Shabbos which will demonstrate the broad range of activities that this *melacha* includes:

1) Many people have sinks with one handle that controls both the hot and cold water. It is forbidden to turn the handle to any direction except all the way to the right, because otherwise hot water will come out. Therefore, when one wants water for *Netilas Yodayim*, he must be **very careful not to pick the handle straight up** even if he will immediately push it to the right [see diagram]. The reason is that while it is in the middle a little water comes out from the hot side, even though it is not hot anymore, and that causes cold water to go into the boiler and get cooked! *(S.S.K. 1:39)

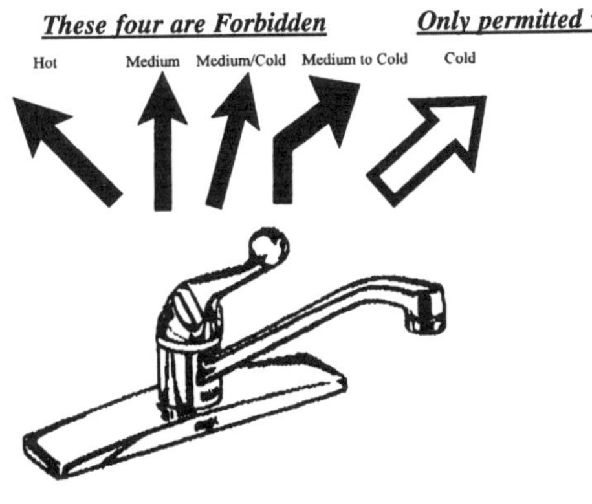

2) If one washed a cup with cold water and there are still drops of water in it (that is, it was not dried), then it is forbidden to pour hot water (from an urn) into the cup since those drops will get cooked. [If, however, the drops are from water that was cooked or drops from a previous cup of tea, and there is not a lot of liquid in the cup, then one can be lenient and pour hot water on it]. (H.S. p. 295)

3) One may not cook something that was baked. Therefore, one may not put *baked* croutons, soup nuts, challah or matzoh into a bowl of

---

* One can avoid this problem by shutting off the hot water to the faucet before Shabbos (there is usually a knob under the sink for this).

soup that was poured from a pot (because, since it is a *kli sheni*[§], it is considered cooking) (H.S. p. 263 and Shabbos Kitchen p. 38).

4) Likewise, one may not bake or roast something that was previously cooked. Therefore, one may not put a piece of *cooked or boiled* chicken (or the like) on top of a pot on the *blech** to warm up because it is now getting roasted [however, if it was *roasted or baked*, then it is permitted to heat it up on top of a pot] (M.B. 318:41 and S.S.K. 1:60).

5) One may not take cold food, even if it is fully cooked or roasted, and put it on the actual *blech*, even for a moment, if it could get *yad soledes bo*** (110°F) if it would stay there the entire day (O.C. 318:14 and *I.M. O.C. I:94*). [Concerning **returning** food to a *blech* see further.]

6) One should be careful not to let any uncooked vegetables or their juices touch any hot solid food on the plate, because solid food retains its *kli rishon*[§] status as long as it is *yad soledes bo*. For example, one should not serve cholent with coleslaw or cucumber salad if the vegetables or juice will touch the hot meat or potatoes of the cholent (M.B. 318:78 and S.S.K. 1:58, see *also Ma'or Hashabbos* 8.9).

7) It is forbidden to stir a pot of hot food if it is not fully cooked, *even* if the pot has been removed from the fire. One should not stir a pot of food while it is on the fire (or on a *blech* directly over the fire), even if it *is* fully cooked. And, since taking out food from a pot usually stirs it, one should not even remove food from a pot that is fully cooked unless he first removes it from the fire (or the part of the *blech* over the fire) (O.C. 318:18 and M.B. 117; and H.S. p. 282).

8) One may not cover a pot of food that is not fully cooked. Therefore, if one lifts the cover of the cholent to see if it is done (or just to smell it) and realizes that it is not completely done, he may not put the cover back on, even if the pot is not on the fire. If, however, the cholent is completely done then he may put the cover back on, but must make sure that any drops on the bottom of the cover are still warm, or they should be shaken off (M.B. 254:23; S.S.K. 1:35 and note 94).

---

§   A *kli rishon* is a pot in which food was cooked on the fire. A *kli rishon* (or equivalent) cooks everything that was not already cooked. A *kli sheni* is a container that the food was poured into from a *kli rishon*, which only cooks certain things.

*   A *blech* is a piece of metal that covers the flame, and preferably also the knobs. A *blech*, being an unusual way of cooking, serves as a reminder not to raise the flame (*I.M. O.C.I:93*).

**   *Yad soledes bo* literally means [a degree of heat that] causes one to withdraw his hand for fear of being burnt. The *Gemara* (*Shabbos* 40b) says that this is the temperature at which a liquid is considered cooked.

9) One may not return the inset (which holds the cooking food) of a crockpot to the base on Shabbos unless the base was lined with aluminum foil or the like (which serves as a *blech*; preferably, the knob also should be covered) (Shabbos Kitchen p. 60).

10) If one took a pot off the fire (or *blech*) on Shabbos, it cannot be returned unless all of the following five conditions are met:

    1) the fire must be covered (with a *blech* or the like)

    2) the food must be fully cooked

    3) the food must still be warm

    4) it was taken off with intention to return it

    5) it was held the entire time (putting it on a counter or table while holding it is acceptable) (O.C. 253:2, M.B. 54 and S.S.K. 1:18).

[See *S.S.K.* 1:19 for when these last two conditions may not be required.]

Chapter 6

The following are some common applications for different *melachos*:

1) You cannot comb your hair on Shabbos [because it will certainly pull out a hair] (O.C. 303:27). However, you may fix your hair a little with your fingers or with a brush if all of the following conditions are met:

> a) the brush has soft bristles that will not pull out **your** hair
>
> b) the brush is set aside for use only on Shabbos
>
> c) you will not use it forcefully or excessively (S.H. p. 163).

2) It is forbidden to bite off a nail. (One has to be very careful if he has a habit of doing this during the week!) It is also forbidden to cut or pull off a nail (O.C. 340:1 and M.B. 1).

3) It is forbidden to pick or pull off a pimple, wart or blister [even if it does not bleed] ! It is likewise forbidden to bite off loose skin on one's lips. This may even be a Biblical prohibition (S.H. p. 160-161).

4) It is forbidden to put **any** water or saliva on a stain on a garment, even if it is embarrassing to wear it like that. **Even one drop** of water or saliva, on a tiny stain, is a violation of this *melacha*! (M.B. 302:46 and S.S.K. 15:24).

5) One may not rub a stain off his clothing by rubbing one part of the garment on the stained part. For example, if there is a stain on your jacket, you may not take your sleeve and rub it out, nor may you use your fingernail to remove it (S.H. p. 179).

6) If *moist* dirt is on one's garment, he may not remove it unless a stain will remain. Therefore, if cholent foll on one's dress, she may remove only the upper layer of the stain (the cholent) with either the back of a knife, a dry cloth or her fingernail, as long as there romains a stain on that place. One may not use a brush or rub the garment vigorously, nor may any water be used (S.S.K. 15:27 and S.H. p. 180).

7) If water spills on the tablecloth [and, likewise, if some liquid spilled on your clothing or it got wet in a rainstorm], you may not use a towel or the like to squeeze the liquid out of the tablecloth. You may clean off the water on the surface by putting a towel, rag or paper towel on it without pressing it down, so that you will not be squeezing it out (S.S.K. 12:38 and S.H. p. 183).

8) It is forbidden to put on **any** cosmetics on Shabbos, whether facial powder, blush, eye make-up, lipstick or nail polish, even clear nail polish (O.C. 303:25 and S.S.K. 14:57-59). [Although it is true that R' Moshe Feinstein *zt"l* (I.M. O.C. I:114) permitted throwing white talc powder on one's face because it does not last (adhere) at all, he writes explicitly that for a woman to color her face is **forbidden**].

9) One may not pull out a loose thread from a garment, whether it is a thread from a hem that became loose, threads left over from a button that fell off, or just a broken thread (S.S.K. 15:68 and *Kitzur Hilchos Shabbos* Ch. 24). It is also forbidden to pull a thread to tighten a stitch or a loose button (S.S.K. 15:67).

10) It is forbidden to make a tight double knot even if you intend to leave it tied only for a few minutes. It is permitted to make a bow-knot. However, if it is intended to stay that way for more than 24 hours it is forbidden. Therefore, if you need to tie a bumper to a crib, or if there is a decorative bow on a dress that is not usually untied, it is forbidden to tie them with a bow-tie unless you intend to undo them within 24 hours (*Ramoh* 317:1, M.B. 317:29 and S.H. p. 224).

11) It is forbidden to tie a single knot at the end of a bag (e.g., to bunch up a storage bag and tie its end into a knot to secure it) [as in the picture at right] regardless of how long it will stay intact. Also, it is forbidden to untie a bag that has been tied in this manner! Instead one may rip it open in a destructive manner [provided that there are no letters or pictures where he tears] (S.H. p. 222).

12) Therefore, if one wants to close a trash bag on Shabbos, it is forbidden to make a double knot or even a bow knot. It is also forbidden to bunch up the top of the bag and tie it into a single knot. What can be done?

    a) make a slip knot (which is not halachically a knot)

    b) take the two ends of the top of the bag and tie them into a single knot [like the first stage of a bow-knot used on shoes] (although it won't be a tight knot, which is why it is permitted, it will still keep the bag closed if it is not moved)

    c) use a plastic strip that you pull through a hole in the strip to tighten (involves no tying)

    d) take a twist-tie and *wrap* it tightly around the bunched up neck of the bag (this also involves no tying) [according to some, you may *twist* a twist-tie, too] (S.H. p. 222).

13) Any knot that one may not tie, he may not tighten. Therefore, it is forbidden to tighten the knot of one's *tzitzis* (S.S.K. 15:50).

14) It is also forbidden to tape two things together. However, concerning tape there is a leniency: if the taping is done temporarily, then it is permitted. Therefore, it is permitted to put on a disposable diaper with its adhesive tapes, but one **must** unfasten the tape when taking the diaper off (not just slip it off). Also, it is **forbidden to fasten the tapes to the diaper when disposing of it** [because then it will be permanent] (S. H. p. 72-74).

15) If one has a pet that is not totally used to living in the house, or it is rebellious, that is, it would want to escape if the door was open, there could be a serious problem of *Tzod* [trapping - one of the *melachos*] when the door of the house is open and you want to close it. (If it is totally domesticated then there is no problem of *Tzod*.)

    The way to avoid this is: if there are two doors, one inside the other, make sure that the first door is closed before the second one is opened; another way is to open the door just enough for you to get out and to block the entire opening of the door while leaving and immediately close the door [this way it is as if the animal has been trapped continuously, avoiding a violation of *Tzod*] (S.S.K. 27:36-37).

16) It is forbidden to smear any cream or ointment. Included in this is hand cream, Vaseline, Desitin [toothpaste (*I.M. O.C.* I:112)] and anything of a similar consistency. One may also not smooth them out on a bandage. However, if ointment is necessary then one is permitted to dab it on to the body (i.e. the wound or the rash) itself, without smearing it at all (Shabbos Kitchen p. 179).

17) It is forbidden to make any letter, picture or meaningful symbol whether on a permanent surface [like paper] or on a temporary surface [such as the fog on a window] (M.B. 340:22 and 20). It is also forbidden to carve a meaningful shape out of food; therefore, one cannot carve a watermelon into the shape of a basket (S.H. p. 12).

18) It is forbidden to read any business related material on Shabbos. Included in this is any bill, receipt or bank statement, as well as any merchandise catalogs or business advertisements (even in the *Yated, Hamodia* or Jewish Observer). [Since the likelihood of reading forbidden material is so great, some *poskim* prohibit reading any newspaper on Shabbos. It is therefore desirable not to

read newspapers at all on Shabbos] (S.S.K. 29:46-47 and S.H. p. 54 and 59).

19) One may not reattach or reinstall a door, window or screen that came off its hinge or out of its track, nor may one remove it (S.S.K. 23: 32; Binyan Shabbos I: p. 7).

20) If a doorknob came out, it is forbidden to put it back (even loosely). If you cannot open the door, you may use a screwdriver or the like to open and close it, but **not** the doorknob (S.S.K. 23: 32).

21) If one's shoelaces came out or ripped, he may put them back in if they are easy to put in (either because the holes are big or the shoelaces have plastic tips), but he may not insert new shoelaces. Neither may he insert shoelaces into a new shoe because that completes them. Similarly, one may not put in a belt that is designated for a specific dress or coat for the first time on Shabbos (O.C. 317:2 and M.B. 16 and 18; and S.S.K. 15:60 and 62).

22) It is forbidden to carry a handkerchief on Shabbos just like anything else; therefore, it may not be carried in one's pocket or tucked under a bracelet. A handkerchief may be taken in the streets only if it is worn in a way that it serves as a scarf or as a belt (instead of one's regular belt). (S.S.K. 18:47-48)

23) An item that by its very nature is neither a utensil nor food, is not considered "prepared" for Shabbos and is therefore *muktzeh*. This type of *muktzeh*, called *muktzeh machmas gufo*, may not be moved at all on Shabbos. Included in this category of *muktzeh* are: a rock, coin, pet or any inedible food, like flour or raw potatoes. Likewise, a flowerpot (with a plant inside) or tree branch may not be moved at all (*M.B.* intro. to *O.C.* 308; *S.S.K.* 20:28 and 26:2; and Halachos of *Muktza* p. 118).

24) Your conversation on Shabbos should not be like your conversation during the week. Therefore, you may not say that after Shabbos you are going to do something which is forbidden to do on Shabbos. For example, you may not say: "I am going to buy this tomorrow," or "I am driving to the city tomorrow." However, you may say "I am *going* to the city tomorrow" (O.C. 307:1 and S.S.K. 29:66).

לעילוי נשמת

ר' שלום בן ר' ארי' לייבוש פויגעל זלל"ה

אוהב שלום ורודף שלום
אהוב לבריות ונערץ מאד על כל מכיריו
רבים נהנו ממנו עצה ותושיה
תרם מהונו להחזקת תלמידי חכמים
ובניית מקומות תורה ותפילה
הרביץ תורה לרבים לעת שיבתו בעמל ובגבורה
נלב"ע ביום י' תמוז תשנ"ט

ולעילוי נשמת אשתו

מרת רבקה רחל בת ר' אהרן פויגעל ע"ה

אצילת נפש ומיוחדת במידותיה הנעלות
נודעת בצדקת פזרונה לתורה וצדקה
סייעה בהקמת מוטדות תורה חינוך וחסד ובהחזקתם
היתה אוזן קשבת לנזקקים בעזרה וסיוע
צנועה היתה בהליכותיה ודרכיה
עטרת בעלה ותפארת משפחתה
ומסורה בלב ונפש לבניה
נלב"ע ביום כ"ד טבת תשס"ב

ת.נ.צ.ב.ה.

In memory of Mr. and Mrs. Shalom Fogel
Whose dedication to Torah and Chesed
Earned them the respect and admiration of all

לעילוי נשמת

אבי מורי ר׳ דוד בן צבי הכהן ז״ל

by
Abbe Kaplan

לעילוי נשמת

אבי מורי ר׳ ליטמן בן חיים דוב בער ז״ל
ואמי מורתי רות רבקה לאה בת אברהם ז״ל

by
Malkiel Nechamkin

Dedicated to the loving Memory of

Robert Troy ע״ה
ר׳ ראובן בן משה ז״ל טרוי

5 Elul 5744

איזהו מכובד המכבד את הבריות
Who is honored, he who honors others

and

Sidney Silver ע״ה
ר׳ שכנא בן קלמן מאיר ז״ל סילבר

8 Tishrei 5753

Our devotion and understanding of our heritage
was instilled in us by our parents. They will always
be remembered with great love and affection.

Joanna and Michael Silver & Family